VOLUME 1

THE EASE OF
CORPORATE
GOVERNANCE

BUSINESS SIMPLIFIED

Written by Prasad Prakash Tupache

(I)

ISBN - 9798880124961

Price

Publishing Year: 2024

Published and Printed By

Independently Published Through Amazon Kindle Direct Publication

Office Address: Amazon (India) Brigade Gateway, 8 Th Floor, 26/1, Dr. Raj Kumar Road , Malleshwaram (W) ,
Bangalore – 560055
Phones: +918033273000
E-mail : amznindpr@amazon.com
Website: www. Amazon.in

Printed in India& Various International Amazon Marketplace (Website) Through Print on Demand Technology

(II)

(III)

ABOUT THE AUTHOR

Author : Mr. Prasad P. Tupache ,

Address: Survey No 79/20,

Shivratna Colony , Pachpir Chauk,

Kokane Nagar, Kalewadi ,

Pimpri, Pune – 411017

Font Setting :   **Publisher** : Amazon KDP

Mr. Prasad P. Tupache .

Cover Design :

Mr. Prasad P. Tupache .

Photo Courtesy :

Front Page : Green and Beige Simple T (Canva.com)

Rear Page : Canva.com

Created From : Canva.com

BLESSINGS

Image Courtesy: Unfold memory, Unsplash.com

Namaste Friends,

Greetings to all of you! Morya!

Every creation is wonderful experience of presenting the knowledge, skill and experience in unique way with the readers engaged with you! Listening to you! Learning with you!

This journey of professional and personal progress is always rewarding and the inner satisfaction one get after completion of a creative project is immense and it makes us happy and content thoroughly!

The Blessings of Bappa are always with us whenever we try to write for a noble cause!

When we are trying to write something useful for others and good for our own comprehension the joy of sharing knowledge get doubled and this real success of attaining knowledge upgrade can be easily sensed through our changed approach to look towards challenges and deal with the obstacles creatively and happily! One time and all time!

Business world is fully creative and to remain in the business for long time one has to constantly think high and achieve big with their efforts and dedication! The inspiration to think comes from the study and qualifications on the basis of which we come to know the various relations of natural entities and how they support or oppose each other during the process! Once we know the relation, we try to establish the interdependence and hence get an equation which drives that relation!

Friends, whenever we get stuck somewhere, we get annoyed and create negative attributes which are not good for us!

The ability to focus on issues with open

Mind and broad heart needs certain plan with which these challenges can be addressed in structured way!

That's what creativity and productivity work together to provide us much needed effectiveness! Once we become effective, later on we become efficient which in turn boost up our capacity and hence make our progress easy and steady!

Throughout this exciting journey, we always seek blessings of Bappa and urge them to provide us the required intellect, needed carefulness and fun loving atmosphere with which we can express us through right words and best spirit!

In this project also, we would try to present the best business concepts in easiest and simplest manner so that the theme line of the project – The Ease of Corporate Governance – can be related easily with simplified business operations and overall dynamics! **Welcome to Volume 1 !**

Morya! Morya!

DEDICATION

Image Courtesy: Antonio scalogna , Unsplash.com

Every Entrepreneur has a well-crafted dream to start his own venture one day! Putting vision, efforts in action and dealing with innumerous challenges in the path, finally the goal gets accomplished! The much awaited social status of successful entrepreneur is always an icing on cake after such goal fulfillment! We wholeheartedly dedicate this book to every spark in the creative minds of struggling entrepreneurs!

THANK YOU

Image Courtesy : Pete pedroza , Unsplash.com

Friends,

Every creation is an art work and at the same times a knowledge offering in the benefit of its users!

Writing 'The Ease of Corporate Governance 'was a fun and to boost the joy of writing we included relevant images with subject matter!

The images are stock images and taken from websites such as 'Unsplash.com', 'Pixabay.com','Pixel.com'. The name of the image creator is written below the included image! We are grateful for this courtesy!

Thank You!

INSPIRATIONAL

Image Courtesy : Kelly Sikkema , Unsplash.com

(X)

INSPIRATIONAL

Image Courtesy : Leone Venter, Unsplash.com

PREFACE

Hello Friends,

It gives us immense pleasure and joy while writing the preface of this new book – The Ease of Corporate Governance – Business Simplified! Let's look some important aspects of this brief preface!

Every human being has to do some form of work for his or her ultimate presence in this world! By birth, many of us are fortunate to have good supporting and caring family with us which takes care of our upbringing unconditionally ! Family support makes it possible to reach new heights of our goals!

In unfortunate event of not having proper family support and understanding, people have to struggle extremely hard to get the spot they desire in life! Ultimately some achieve their dream while some keep trying till their last breathe! The pursuit for goal is always filled with moments of persistence and courage! People keep fighting till they reach their destinations!

When business world is concerned with regard to historical references, it was always considered as holy work of exchanging scarce resources to each other at its mutually agreed price! The magic of your demand getting fulfilled is so exciting and hilarious that once you get what you need you are ready to pay its price! The price needs to be mutually agreed!

Number of merchants with their sample product stock keeps searching markets for their products! They travel a lot and each travel makes them more knowledgeable and aware about what's happening in various parts of the globe!

Visiting same location within span of six months shows the picture of development happened in that phase of time! It is the vision of that nation and its quest for ultimate upliftment of the society in meaningful manner!

This scene of development is exact choice of any merchant passing that way!

Resourcefulness is everyone's need and authorities are there to ensure people get adequate resources to live their daily live normally and happily! Abundance of resources and shortages of resources, both things are not good for general economic outlook of any region! The reason is that, in case of shortages of resources the prices of that particular product or service keep increasing adding to higher level of inflation! Which create some amount of friction from people side! In other way, abundance of resources reduces the prices of the products which make merchants uncomfortable to get their necessary earnings to run the show in descent manner! So one has to always find a good level of equilibrium with demand and supply of necessary resources!

Global Economy's has several types – some nations are highly capital centric, some relate their economy with income coming from service industries in the terrain; some nation has natural resource oriented economy while

Some deals with extremely poor state of low financial holdings that survival in such environment becomes one of the most difficult task!

Still people live there , they work there , they get some form of education and later on with highest efforts of their hard work they immigrate to some better economies where they get the needed resources almost regularly and at a price they can easily afford to !

This condition of relocating to some better economies has always a challenge of acceptance by lawful permanent residence in that region! Some nations need human resources for their national planned developments and hence they may relax some rules of allowing qualified and talented people from various parts of the globe! They make it quite clear to everyone out there that the proposed development is mutually beneficial and they will always try to provide a soothing workable atmosphere where people can easily work & live happily! This is what the concept of co –living is! Society keeps changing as development keep happening!

Taxes are ways with which any statutory authority charges the amount for their service to people! Its government and government are for people! Government needs a workforce fully qualified for their bigger responsibilities to serve the society and hence every resource needs remuneration for their service to people! The care of this service is taken by government and hence through collection of various duties and taxes government make it sure that incoming and outgoing parts are taxed as per their legitimate tax structure designed by the financial experts present in the national finance board and ministry!

So, every year, people keep up the track of collection of taxes and accordingly decide the next years financial planning and implementation! Annual financial budget is ultimate exercise of deciding various tax rates and allowable exemptions that keep eye on incomes and gross domestic product in total!

Things are simple and easy to understand! Work is a way of engaging resources in some form of intellectual or physical task so as to get desired outcome of that work! You have to make arrangement of people, you have to provide those latest tools and tackles, you have to provide those guidelines and inputs and then you have to give them much needed time to accomplish that work up to desired standards!

Then you will come to see whether the work done is right or wrong! If the work is right, you will accept it and if the work is wrong you will suggest repairing or rectifying it! The person will again devote his time and will start repairing what went wrong! After rectification , the work will be seen and if still it contains error then again the same has to be attended till it get final acceptance !

Friends this is what the work is! Final acceptance of your work is essential before going ahead! This means certain permission is necessary every time you perform a work either to check the work done is right or work done is wrong!

This permission is the ultimate decision whether to go ahead or stop for a while, correct the things which are not right, ponder some thoughts on how we can minimize such mistakes, what we learned from such mistakes, what is the liability of that mistake for any resource or any institution? When we start asking such question to each other in that environment, we come to know about the meaningful ways of working which assist productive outcome of engaged energy and time! This sets the path for system effectiveness and system efficiency!

What effectiveness we ascertain? Effectiveness is the base on which the tower of excellence is created and constructed in any system! We are effective means we can do our work right and we can do our work in given amount of time! Effective means we know what we have to do and we know what we should never do!

Effectiveness means we know after how many efforts the desired outcome will yield and after how many sub attempts it will repeat itself to desired production level! Once this understanding gets created with us, we try to further improve this repeat occurrence!

Our ability to repeat the same desirable or undesirable output again and again and with accurate control of system indicators denotes our skill of performing that particular operation! We are skilled means for day and night; we can do any specific activity with same quality output and without any defects! Skill means achieving the given target in given time and yet keeping it clearly acceptable!

So time and output will always accompany each other! Whenever there will be work, there has to be some time frame! Within that particular time frame the work in hand has to be finished so that next journey step can be attained! As we go on accomplishing each stage of the journey , eventually we meet our last point which is total completion of the work and now the completed work is waiting for its client's final acceptance!

Doing same work again and again with same quality of work gives you experience! Experience is a very very dynamic term as such! It's the complete intellectual development happens for anyone who is carrying out a particular work! While assessing anyone's experience , people tell year of service they served for particular role or task , people enumerate their challenging assignments and their achievements while giving justice to that role, people point out the severity of obstacles in their path and how they overcome it to meet the final much desired goal ! People explain how a special training helped them to overcome the earlier doubts in their mind and now how they are feeling comfortable! People tell us number of situations which were demanding and number of situations which were little bit easy going! Then how they worked in demanding situations and how they developed their overall work related personality in easy going time! This sharing helps to improve effectiveness and efficiency in any system!

So, as people starts telling their experiences of doing that work, people in the system keep listening them, noting them, appreciating them, correcting them and concluding them! The whole aim of telling experience of work is to get understanding of the fact that yes, the work can be done! Work can be done by some special person! Work can be done by any person with special instrument! Work can be done without any person but just by installing necessary automation in the streamline!

Feedbacks are the inputs which are received from different person interacting in the system for various work related activities! When starting an activity , when completing it as per the best suitable requirement and while certifying its completion, people tend to get an internal feeling in their mind about that work! When people finish an assigned work, they usually get satisfied after its desired completion! There is moment of pride associated with that achievement that yes, earlier we were not sure, whether we will achieve it and now as we have achieved it, we are feeling proud full!

The feeling of pride generates sense of self-esteem and in turn builds morale of resources working in the system! This morale keep helping each other and this way the flow of work get transferred from one hand to other hand continuously! This chain of work supply is essential and it ultimately decides the efficiency of your work!

In this team work, you have to ensure that every resource is working as per their role! Every resource is working as they are guided and every resource is working for time allotted to them to finish that work! Knowing these performance limits, people adjust their expertise of doing that work so that they ultimately finish the work within given constraints! In the end, it gets counted for professional team building spirit! People rate each other through a detailed check list and assign performance rank so that one can understand how better the work is done as an individual and as a team!

When the work is done satisfactorily as per internal understanding and as the party for which work is done is accepting that work and providing the mutually agreed price , it's time now to earn the rewards of team's overall contribution !

Rewards from person to whom you served can be monetary , it can be exchange of other useful resources for further service or simply it can be a goodwill generation for future prospectus of working together on long term assignment that prosper equally to both parties constructively !

Over the years same practices are followed to make service of each other comfortable to each other in order to serve for long time!

Obviously, when you are giving money to someone it means someone has to receive it! The mode of payment since historical time followed a strict discipline of personal trust on each other! Maintenance of trust level is first and foremost important duty of partners in agreement of serving each other!

The stories of creating the trust and consolidating the foundation of trust are told very very interestingly in ancient literature through legendary characters! Several international countries travelled each other's region through available trade routes at that time and also as per the discovery of new lands in the pursuit of new market!

We know how the earlier sailors tackled the discovery of new lands when they want to go to different place and in meantime they reached a different place! Before the technological evolution, trade with different nation was a challenging task and high level of intellect was essential to persuade others for the point why they are serving particular service segment and why other should associate with them at that moment and what will happen if they don't associate at all!

Basic level of such type of enquiries laid the foundation of order details and product specifications!

When it is about serving others, it is essential to tell other party how you will serve or other party will put forward the terms of mutually agreed service norms and service standards! Fulfillment of these norms and attaining specified standards proves your commitment to serve in the eyes of other party and then the party does what they are supposed to do when they are totally satisfied with the kind of service they experienced!

This sense of others care laid the strong foundation of customer satisfaction and day by day the concept keeps evolving and later become a widely accepted international norm that if you have to serve something over the entire global region , you have to fulfill the global service standards !

Then various nations independently formed the authentic requirements they expect from a domestic or foreign land's product! The ultimate aims of forming these requirements are safety of their own people during consuming foreign resources and maintaining a monetary equilibrium for the received service!

So again the role of mutual trust and interpersonal relations become essential! As the traders keep traveling various regions, they keep meeting rulers of the territory for mutual trade related and general discussions! During the time of empires, various entrepreneurs and traders started keeping close contacts with the rulers through trustworthy resources!

Rulers were running their states and hence were always held responsible for their people safety and welfare! Hence before meeting any domestic citizen or foreign citizen, rulers initiated some form of assessment of person before starting a discussion! The scrutiny process always helped rulers to have some type of official record on the basis of which the purpose and contribution of the person can be analyzed easily before going ahead with future developments!

This again made the close association of politics and traders! Traders has ability to deliver the products and service required for people of the nation to fulfill their daily needs while politics has ability to allow certain traders

With whom countrymen will receive necessary products and services at reasonably affordable price with respect to national currency! The fundamentals of international trade and business got created through such dealings over the past thousand years!

Technological and scientific developments over last two hundred to three hundred year ago given rise to consumption of certain natural resources like oil, metals and agri products as commodity! Equations of trade of these commodities across the continents derived the directions and improvements in international trade and resource supply!

This development of yester centuries is still going on strongly in present days and higher degree of trade innovations are being researched and applied in market! Advent of mobile applications for trading shares, getting information of various organizations through their official web sites , handling foreign exchange transactions at the click of the mouse or on touch screen of mobile has simply made trade decisions extremely user oriented and superfast!

Growth is the ultimate aim of any trader providing products or services! Historically products are either grown in nature through traditional ways of farming and plantation or they are created inside dedicated establishments! Indian rural life and rural culture was fully equipped with trades that fulfill daily needs of the citizens residing! It means we have farmers, we have potters, we have black smith, we have construction wizard, we have painters, we have decorators, and we have doctors! Since that time, regular need of fulfillment of resources and fulfillment of service to people is well identified and every ruler tried his or her best that his or her state will be a prosperous state having all qualities necessary to live a comfortable and happy life during their tenure!

Then it comes the development of villages to cities and cities to metros! As time evolved and population keeps increasing, demand for resources got doubled and tripled and many times for certain resources, it is quadrupled!

Now in the search of fulfillment of these resources, people don't have any option but either grow the resources in their farms or find them through various excavations till the pursuit is over and it meets that times need! At the same time, in scientific research many new techniques are developed where a reasonably good alternative having low cost and nearly equal usability are discovered to reduce requirement of valuable resource and availability of newly found resource! The precious and scarce resources are used for extremely special purpose at a higher purchase price while standard alternative material serving nearly similar purpose is provided for some less risky purpose!

When production demands for a particular product or service is increased, it was necessary to build required manpower that is skilled and trained to create those products! Thus industrial quest for supply of product given rise to establishment of major technical institutes in the world! These institutes served to deliver competence required to perform an industrial role! Again various institutes keep excelling themselves through close tie up with prominent industrial set ups and they keep providing high caliber students to these industries! The human capital exchange laid the foundation of human resource development and role of Corporate HR in driving business operations!

As development of human resources is supposed to be very very critical for the overall growth of the organization, people invented various up skilling programs so that the manpower can be regularly skilled and trained. This resulted into development of product output and its final quality! Product sales increased, profit increased and customer engagement with the firm also increased!

Observant management of any industrial establishment always lay down its long term vision to achieve the desired growth and ensure business remains in business for longer years! This thinking given rise to have some form of robust systems which will ensure the repeat success and stability inside the organization!

In other words, organizations started to think sustainable business solutions for their customers as well as for their own organizations! All business functions got a deep shock when market behaved unpredictable and aggressive than their expectations and frequent cycles of recession and retrenchment are experienced!

How to survive in such challenging conditions was a billion dollar question in front of board of the directors of multimillionaire organizations where more than ten thousand – twenty thousand people use to serve directly and more than double people are dependent on their existence inside that fraternity!

Knowledge is the ultimate healer and best solution to resolve difficult times! People find out digital platforms where global requirements in any market condition can be assessed and accordingly their production schedules can be modified to ensure there is minimum lying inventory inside their system and a descent product turnaround is achieved which ensures reasonably good profit!

Rise of video communication technology made networking extremely easy and people started using this engineering marvel to communicate their business needs!

According to different organizational structure the hierarchy of requirement is communicated and necessary approvals or denials are recorded! Accordingly material or service purchase is done for the business and its accrued price is paid by the business!

The complete spectrum of any industrial or trade establishments including its internal system of supplying parts as well as external system of demanding parts need to follow a certain discipline , set of rules , code of ethics to ensure the needy product or service is delivered in right time , at right price and with best possible after sales service !

These set of rules formed the foundation of major vigilance system required for any small-medium-big industrial establishment which come to known as "Corporate Governance! "

So who will monitor whom! Who will report whom! Who will hire whom! Who will fire whom! Who will contribute to organization and whose contribution is ideally valued by the organization! All these questions are answered through dedicated matrix of corporate governance!

Rules are rules and people don't like rules! These are two extremely opposite working conditions essential to run the show in presentable manner! Every business house has to find a way out between how many rules are extremely important to drive the business momentum and how many rules are not necessary!

People love freedom and adults love it most! They know why they come to office every day and what they are expected to deliver! Line managers and divisional managers are totally aware that what is required run rate of this month and how the team is playing! What kinds of changes are required to make this team play a rapid and profitable game! The supreme management and the boards of the directors are always planning for multidirectional growth of the organization in next three to five years and accordingly they are busy in discussions with various governments and authorities who can understand their business potential and opportunities of national employment and hence contribution to gross domestic product!

In corporate governance, everyone has a written assigned role and unwritten job commitment! When things are committed, they have to fulfilled by putting every right effort! The ability to change your present scenario and making it easy for future is the ultimate identity of any corporate star!

Rule with no rule is the best governance !To achieve such a high level of degree of freedom in the organization , everyone need to accept the total responsibility of success and failure on their own after complete review and assessment of any happening inside or outside the organization ! Once accountability is set, one has to correct it, avoid the same in next try and ensure everyone know the same to avoid further repetition!

This book will talk on informal ways of achieving good corporate governance to simplify business! This book will talk on important business practices in current times which attract the customer attention and retain his enhanced trust on your deliverables! This book talks on different behaviors of customers and how as an ethical and professional organization you are supposed to respond to certain challenges! This book will talk on importance of personal values and business values and how both value systems need to be same to define the ultimate nature of the business! This book will talk on opportunities and how to make most benefit out of them! This book will talk on why corporate governance is necessary and what will happen if corporate governance fails! This book will talk on external business image and its linking to shareholders interest as well as stakeholder's interest! This book will talk on the idea of market trends and how business has to respond to a certain trend with maintaining requirements of corporate governance!

In the end, every business has to serve a larger society need and while serving society they have to ensure their existence by earning descent profits! The generation of business balance sheets is ultimate account of annual business performance and corporate governance has deep thought and quick action in ensuring balance sheet shows good profit after tax and depreciation of its assets and least liability on the sides of loans and inventory lying which descends the growth trajectory!

The image of the business is supreme and in corporate governance everyone is trained to do their role is descent way so as business image remain clean and productive! Illusion of trust in the eyes of customer and stakeholder is harmful for business and hence role of business confidentiality and business transparency is equally challenging now a days!

We hope, this book **Volume 1** will simplify the major concepts of corporate governance to make sure you understand a simplified business model which is clear and stable ! Thanks!

INDEX

INDEX

WE ARE OPEN NOW!

VOLUME 1

THE EASE OF
CORPORATE
GOVERNANCE

BUSINESS SIMPLIFIED

Written by Prasad Prakash Tupache

(A-X)

CHAPTER 1: BUSINESS PURPOSE

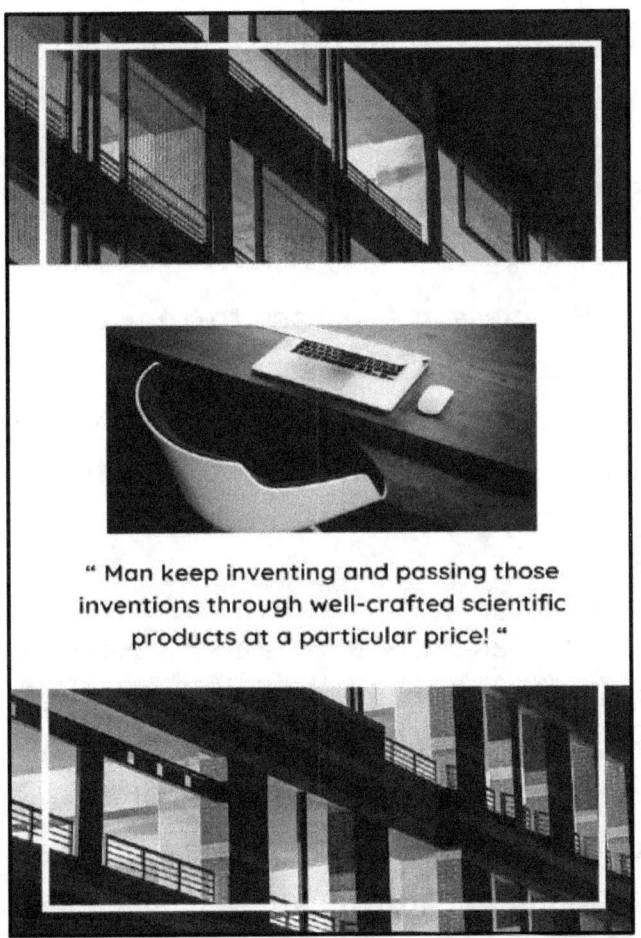

" Man keep inventing and passing those inventions through well-crafted scientific products at a particular price! "

Image Courtesy: Luca Bravo , Unsplash.com

1.1 Introduction:

Hello Friends, Namaste!

Starting the book on Corporate Governance is always much awaited understanding that this is important subject matter and we have to present it in most simplest manner so that anyone who will read this book , will quickly able to understand the basics of corporate governance !

Business means act to remain busy! As simple as that! There are various ways with which one can remain busy! All those ways are commercialized to provide us ultimate outcome of said busy-ness which are known as products and services!

Created products and offered services have a value attached to them in practical day to day market! This value is combination of material consumed, manpower engaged, machines used, maintenance charges paid, modern manufacturing methods used etc. which ultimately meet to overall costing of the product which has direct costing and indirect costing like administrative cost , printing cost , service &

utility bills and so on ! Then the expected profit is added to arrive at a final value of that product or service which is known as its sales price! As per the legal laws of the land, every product or service is charged with its applicable tax! So sales price get increased when tax component is added! Further to this, if transportation charges are there, they also get added to final customer! Thus total value of providing that product at customers address come up with total cost plus profit plus taxes plus carrier charges! Combined total of all these components form an amount which is payable by that customer for availing the product or service! This value is known as purchase price! It is the exact amount which customer has to ultimately pay to procure that product or service!

Every product or service is offered to customer as per some agreed rules and regulations of supply! These terms are mutually agreed or producer may set a clause in which they can request customer to read all purchase instruction before product being purchased! This is how professional work is delivered!

1.2 Need of Business:

Since ancient times, human race is surviving with the help of natural and man-made resources to lead a healthy and happy life! Starting from stone age , moving to copper age , further moving to steel age and now in e- age human race developed themselves through continuous quest of curiosity and scientific application to nearby natural phenomenon's !

Inventions created magic of transforming human lives in following ways:-

1) Inventions created feeling of group study of natural phenomenon!
2) Inventions given trust and confidence to society that something creative and useful can be delivered by team of experts at reasonable price so that life can become easy!
3) Inventions reduced human efforts through creation of machines, equipment's and gazettes! All are serving for luxury and comfort of mankind!
4) If inventions would not have happened, human race may have struggled to make their life easy!

Image of Invention:

Image courtesy: Maria Teneva, Unsplash.com

1.2.1 Commercial Benefit of Inventions:

The hard work behind every invention was necessary to be paid back to its inventors and producers in the form of monetary amount! This amount per piece is decided on the basis of several factors which includes –need of that part , its manufacturing cost , its intellectual efforts , its durability , its scarcity and accordingly a value is derived to sale that product to needy customer !

Once the product usability is proved, the product got its demand from major part of the world initially which later spread to complete globe! This way the inventors formed establishments where these products can be prepared in huge scale to fulfill the need of the customer and ultimately sale those items so that monetary rewards are achieved! This act of exchanging created product or service with respect to its value given birth to business!

Birth of Business:

Image courtesy: Ian Schnieder, Unsplash.com

Once the business birth took place, many inventors started their business to create scientific products that meet human need and started selling throughout globe consistently!

1.2.2 Various Business Needs:

Since pre historical times, human race was always striving hard to get good food, good shelter and good clothing! The three basic necessities of life improved to their ease of availability as the years of human development keep passing!

People started construction of house earlier made up of mud and wooden parts! This idea further developed to house with metallic parts! In current times, house is built with solid RCC structure and which is fully technology friendly having arrangement of CCTV cameras and Do not disturb places specifically accommodated!

Similarly, food business development keeps happening! As human race approached towards further progress new corps is discovered and their yield is gathered for human benefits! Starting from traditional farming to moving into bio technology era, science has given huge contribution to provide ample food resources to present manpower in the global outset! This is noteworthy task!

Third basic human need clothing have interesting story! Earlier people used to cover themselves with very few clothes which are mostly made up of various protective natural tree leaves! This is further improved to cotton clothes, silk clothes! As textile industry excelled in their fabric inventions, new hybrids are discovered and provided to customer! This development given rise to invention of polyester, denim jeans, linen etc.! The comfort of wearing a fabric is always desirable and accordingly customer needs are fulfilled!

Man keep inventing and passing those inventions through well-crafted scientific products at a particular price! This typical exchange of product and service to proposed customer or client through globe highlighted need of doing business and people keep moving to each other nation to look for bigger business opportunities and co-operation ties!

The give and take principle of business got matured with earning of profit and hence people worked hard to change their lives with the help of many business ideas over the past thousand years of human revolution! ✳✳✳

CHAPTER 2: BUSINESS VALUES

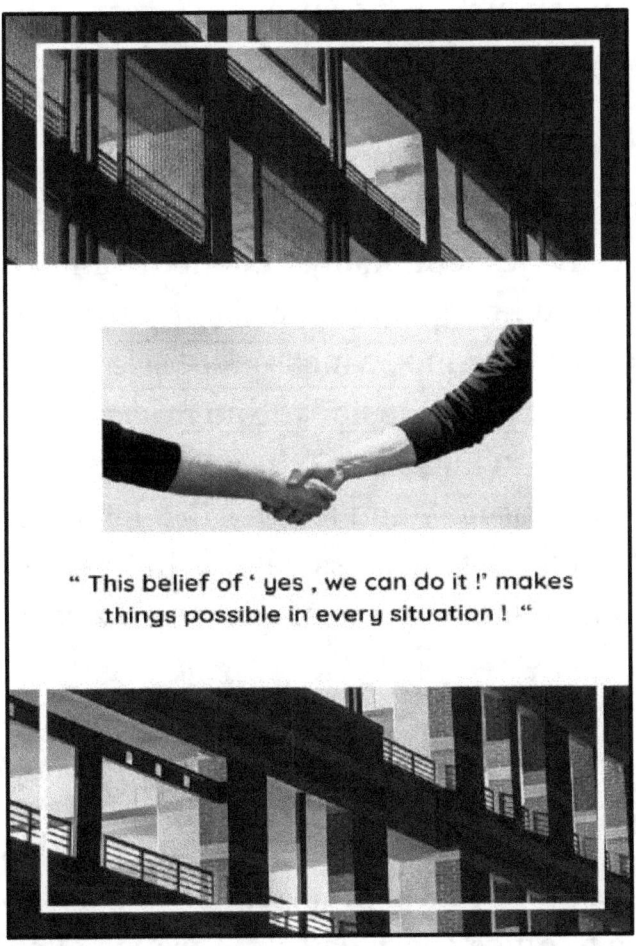

"This belief of 'yes, we can do it!' makes things possible in every situation!"

Image Courtesy: Chris Liverani , Unsplash.com

2.1 Introduction:

Hello Friends,

Every business starts with a business Idea! Business idea is the brain child of an entrepreneur! Entrepreneur can be an experienced professional in several fields, he can be a die-hard problem solver, she can be a superb communicator or they can be a group of technocrats who are highly service friendly! So basically exceptionally talented and deeply grounded people enters into the field of entrepreneurship which give rise to various business clusters inside the huge society to serve humanity to make this world a best place to live and love for now and forever ! So let's see, some of the driving business values that really define the all-round progress of any organization!

2.2 Why are we in the business - Purpose:

At the forefront of anything , this first value is very much important as it inspire you to come to office every day and through all its dark and thin !

2.3 Belief of Business system:

Business is teamwork and hence team need to have positive and driving belief system which always push you to touch the unknown ! Challenge the status quo and build systems that make difference in the society in huge scale ! This belief of ' yes , we can do it !' makes things possible in every situation !

2.4 Market Knowhow – Business Curiosity :

Ultimately when we are creating products and services , it means we are targeting particular purchasers who can avail those services or offering from our side ! So , markets can be specific, special, regular, niche , huge , waste, large , remote , monotonous , capitalist , export , delicate , knowledge driven , emergency related or simply funful ! What kind of market and what kind of market size you are serving is always important to bring your business forward ! One can enter in particular market and later can develop themselves into several nearby or altogether different markets ! This development is market reach !

2.5 Financial Acumen – Business Transparency:

Businesses handle bulk finance in the range of several lakhs to several crores ! The person instructing and guiding about financial dealings to every team member and authorized person need to be extremely clever and brave to give those permissions! Taking money and receiving money as well as maintaining required liquidity and capital in the business system is the skill of prudent business leader!

2.6 Technical Know-How : Base of Engineering :

Modern businesses are more about use of specific resources to reduce human efforts ! Excellent technical know-how saves product preparation cost , saves time of designing - manufacturing and installation and it saves manpower efforts and costs ! One can achieve excellent engineering knowledge by trying different experiments as pilot project and studying their effects in dedicated research labs where same can be commercialized later on !

2.7 Seller to Facilitator Approach :

Business is not only about selling , it is about making your customer more and more comfortable about your presentation , your products , your manufacturing systems , your people , your service standards, your philosophy , your pricing openness and your overall facilitation from customer entering your premises to long term functioning of your products ! Ultimately , if purchased product doesn't give the desired result , then investment made by customer eventually goes in vain !

2.8 Truth – Trust – Tides : Business Excellence :

Business has to stand strong when incidences of presenting truth of technical challenges, trust of remote installation operations and tides of transportation need to be proved ! In short , right from initiating the business activity till its delivery to customer premises , a clear flow of document accompany finish good so that identification and traceability can be cross checked at any point , anytime!

2.9 Business Dynamics – Strength Factor :

One has to be strong and smart enough to sense and act according to market changes, financial changes and manpower requirements ! In business , problems come and wait for your action till you don't take required action ! It is as simple as that ! So , more proactive planning you do for your anticipated business challenges , more easily and quickly you surpass that phase and can focus on regular business activities which records sales and profits after serving your customers and clients!

2.10 Business Ownership – My feel :

One of the most sought after skill of any businessman is his or her ability to own the business success as well as business failures with calm mind and take appropriate steps so as to drive business forward ! Backward path in business are highly expensive and they reduce morale of the team ! To imbibe faith in people , you have to balance ownership with respect to duties and its accountability ! It takes time but ownership is the foundation of business !

2.11 Break Even point of satisfaction :

Every business is done for growth and satisfaction! In business you have to purchase many things as well as you have to sell many things ! In between , you are converting raw material into useful products that meets human needs ! So , to fulfill those needs correctly , we have to do accurate work and ensure more work can be done in same fashion to serve most of them knowing our potential and limit! So , as a business leader , attaining the break-even point of business satisfaction is the first and foremost concern to build a highly performing team !

2.12 Social Connect – Empathy- Brotherhood- Educational Efforts :

Generations keep growing and learning when a business gets started in the region ! The pupils of staff and workmen inculcate life values from their parents which in turn acquire those values from where they are working and where they are living ! Environment has great effect on society development and businesses can contribute to society through regular social connect emphasizing empathy for others and keenness to build feeling of brotherhood as well as interest to learn and grow ! More such resources will be provided by the businesses , more local talent will get flourish in future!

2.13 Spirit of the business – Development :

Successful businesses constantly innovate, experiment , discuss , apply and review changes . It makes them future ready and active to adapt happenings around them easily and regularly ! Development gets multifold expansion when great vision works to design it!

2.14 Longevity :

Business is long term activity and business can last for 200-300 years based on customer trust and product features ! Hope , the business values are discussed properly ! ⊛⊛⊛

CHAPTER 3: BUSINESS ETHICS

" More critical the product need, customer will pay its price! "

Image Courtesy: Razvan Chisu , Unsplash.com

3.1 Introduction:

Hello Friends,

We are now moving towards yet another important aspect of corporate governance which is known as business ethics!

Ethics , as we all know , are some of the good habits , good gestures, good behavior , good practice that ensure whatever we do or perform will yield good outcome in any situation , in any surrounding and at any time ! The complete integrity of corporate governance is gauged with respect to practical experience of business ethics nurtured and followed by the organization since inception of the organization till current journey which can be of ten years, twenty years, fifty years or hundred years! You travel through progressive path because you follow your business ethics! Let's see, some of the basic business ethics which are followed by successful business houses and let's also see which are malpractices which are harmful for business to have long term presence! Understanding of ethics along with malpractices will provide clear picture of right culture inside and outside the organization!

1) Certifications are identity of your business systems! Regular upgrade of certification indicates relevance of system with respect to changes in business world which keep happening regularly!

2) Debit and credit are two fundamental business transactions which are mathematical equations! You have to match business tally in all transactions! More clean is the total, better financial indicators can be understood !

3) Debt is just a support system for initial business momentum! One must try to do business with least debt amount as you have to repay the debt with interest agreed, which directly get cut through your profits!

4) Designs need to be simple and productive! Simple designs consume less manpower and business energy! You have to balance technical requirements and skill availability to ensure your designs produce required output regularly!

5) Human capital is priceless! Good business houses take good care of human capital through their regular training & development, appraisals, increments, medical assistance, job security, social support! Every penny invested in human capital creates a forward pass energetic work culture! Basically people have some basic needs and when they get fulfilled firmly they put more efforts to maintain the scene forever!

6) Conflicts happen everywhere! They have to be resolved with calm mind! Right form of root cause analysis and necessary corrective action resolves the current conflict! To avoid repetition in future, you have to devise a better preventive solution after discussion with group!

7) Profits may not be regular, salaries need to be! Right form of salary structure ensures you pay when it needs to be paid!

8) Business liabilities can be short term, medium term and long term! Successful businesses balance repayment of their liabilities and ensure they get good credit when they repay their liabilities! On the basis of business credit, assurance is set for the firm that every penny will be paid!

9) If you want to do business for five years, you must have range of diverse products which get sold! Your product basket can be – Low profit - high volume, Medium profit – regular demand, High profit – Less demand! This combination will ensure you serve different customers same time managing your production activities in dedicated facilities for every customer need!

10) More critical the product need, customer will pay its price! To create critical products, you have to acquire latest technical expertise! People try to find domestic production sources first, when they are not available, then they look for import markets!

11) Facilities ensure speedy operations! You have to install easy and safe business facilities which make people and part movement rapid and safe! Always take care of infrastructure, connectivity, business network, loading-unloading, check in – check outs!

12) Business needs food, water and relaxation! Ensure people find right type of work-life balance when they are associated with you and also parted from you! In both scenarios, you have to maintain professionalism!

13) What will happen if this mistake is repeated? Always create a culture where errors and mistakes are noted and right guidance is done so that it will not repeat on regular basis! Mistake proofing methods ensure system is pro- active!

14) Vision of the business is long term planning while mission of the business is step by step encounter!

15) Equity market responds to business changes! Response can be bullish or sluggish! Investment and disinvestment are major concern of top business leaders! When your internal systems are robust, business outcome is almost stable and it can be predicted easily! Higher level of business prediction ensures more trust of investors! Investors can work out actual target time for which they can invest regularly!

16) Business may experience sudden shocks or abrupt booms! While carrying out business planning, both these scenarios need to be taken into account to deal with the situations swiftly! When business experience shocks, you have to place shock proof mechanism that will help and when business experience boom, you have to take its maximum benefit!

17) Customer's satisfaction is related to total service offering through technical grip!

18) Whether you are doing business today or ten years later, records keep you active in the court of justice and law! Audits, surveillance, feedbacks have its own importance! Always maintain records on regular basis! As soon as physical action gets completed, its documented identification is must in the business!

19) Repair, replacement and rectification indicate your service readiness in-house or outside business facilities! When tackling outside business challenges, you have to abide by relevant rules!

20) Business will survive till business plan is promising! A promising business plan is outcome of orders in hand! Your marketing efforts are result of your design capabilities and manufacturing excellence!

21) Stay legally safe in all situations! Business is legal form of exchange of goods and service at a set price! ✱✱✱

CHAPTER 4: GOVERNMENT REGULATIONS

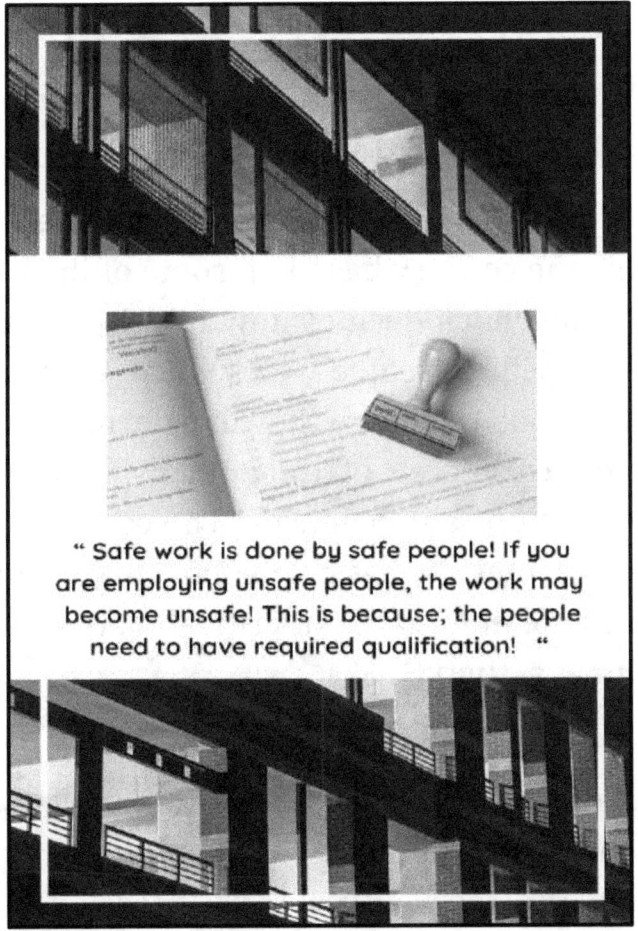

" Safe work is done by safe people! If you are employing unsafe people, the work may become unsafe! This is because; the people need to have required qualification! "

Image Courtesy: Markus Spiske , Unsplash.com

4.1 Introduction:

Hello Friends,

In this chapter, we are going to see how government regulations decide the actual functioning of corporate governance!

4.2 Government: A Universal Set –U:

Every country has their own government to rule the country based on some of the laws of the lands which decides how the citizens of the country will be treated with justice, equality and brotherhood to ensure they live normal life with abundance degree of freedom by adhering to lawful actions and behavior! The concept of one ness and integrity has prime most importance as well as confidentiality of critical matters is also essential activity!

If a country is taken into account, the government can be considered as a universal set which has space for citizens, businesses, schools, transport, agriculture, services and all performing and non performing, visible and invisible assets inside their territory!

So, it can be easily understood that the basic aim of the government is to take care of each of its subsets with equal integrity and solidarity! Government has to stay strong whenever the weaker section of the society is under influence of pressure from other sections of the society. They have to protect individuals by assuring enough opportunities to win their livelihood as well enough freedom to create their careers outside the nation!

A business being one of the regular contributors to economy of the nation, their role in social upliftment is crucial! After government, if someone is creating source of employments in the nation then it's business houses! Opportunities availed by citizens create major changes in their lifestyle! They get regular source of income, they get financial security, and they receive benefits of social recognition and thus a progressive path become visible! So, in order to run the businesses smoothly and also to ensure people are leading a rewarding life, governments forms some business laws which take care of business system and people safety! Let's have a look!

4.3 Safety Regulations:

While running businesses with intention to sell people friendly products, businesses have to follow strict safety norms! In international businesses, we have safety standards and codes of manufacturing which decides most preferred way of a product manufacturing or delivering a service! Business has to provide compliance as defined in the regulation made for safety! Safety regulation has both way advantages! First one is they ensure –you remain safe during product creation, second one – they ensure user and environment remain safe when product is under use or disposed! So, while creating and delivering products and services, complete inspection of facility as well as proper documentation of product creation matching with safety norms is essential! A certificate of acceptance of as observed facility is best indicator of product safety!

4.4 Capacity Regulations:

You have created a facility suitable for certain range of product capacity!

Here, as per natural logic, you can create things which are lower or equal to rated production capacity, if you have to create some other products which exceeds the rated production capacity, then regulation will not allow its creation! You have to either install a nearby special facility and get that facility certified for enhanced capacity and then start its creation or you have to break that capacity into two halves so that same can fall below the previous rated capacity with its customer approval! Capacity regulations not only play vital roles in product creation but transportation-movement- supply also has profound effect on production capacity! E.g. to transport fifty pipes of three meters , a small vehicle is sufficient, however if the OD and Length of the pipe is doubled, we have to book a bigger vehicle!

4.5 Qualification Regulations:

Safe work is done by safe people! If you are employing unsafe people, the work may become unsafe! This is because; the people need to have required qualification!

In business, everyone doesn't need to have a technical qualification but a qualification suggested for that particular role is must to deal with daily challenges easily! That's what the ultimate purpose of the qualification and merit is ! Cleverer the candidate more will be his or her efficiency and fewer problems will arise to ensure business operations run smoothly!

So, when a particular business role is filled, having adequate qualification and experience of that role is utmost important to drive the business smoothly and correctly! Radiography, Dealing with LPG, Explosives, Working nearer harsh chemicals requires certain expertise and qualifications! Businesses have to recruit talent in their organization having these necessary qualifications!

4.6 Market Regulations:

When you are dealing with an international market, then every nation has their typical product or service acceptance system which is governed by international market laws!

Businesses has to ensure, these market regulation are followed and updated regularly! e.g. If there is no trade within two countries for more than one year, before restarting trade with that country , confirmation of all clearances is what expected before entering into fresh business deal ! Some markets accept international certification like CE marking! Any product having CE certification gets access to countries associated with that marking! Some countries need particular inspection agencies to certify the product before packed! If that agencies stamp and certificate is available, then country accepts that material! So, one has to follow such market regulations which makes their products sale possible nationally and internationally!

4.7 Trade treaty regulations:

Over the friendly relation between various nations products can be sold within member countries under different trade treaties! Here both parties get benefit of doing business with each other! Before entering into such trade treaty, business has to comply treaty conditions and they have to receive a no objection certificate from all participated countries in that particular group! Once they carry all formalities, they can trade with member nations and hence a regular trade path get established till the trade treaty is active!

4.8 SEZ regulations:

Special economic zones are created to have global supply of products and services across various regions! Selling products in SEZ region has certain norms and rules! Business houses before starting trading has to attain such clearance certificates with the help of which they can do business in SEZ zone!

4.9 Equity market regulations:

Huge capital is raised through equity market. Business before promoting their shares and going public, they need to comply regulations of stock exchange regulatory board! Many regulations come time to time which business has to follow!

Effect of not following stock market regulations deter business image and business has to lose trust of its investors and also has to suffer financial losses! Its two way sword! Till you are in stock market and your stocks are getting good attention , it's all fine , once you start performing low to your expected standards and business start recording less profit , you lose faith of the investors which expect good returns on their investment and they are always looking for some better investment opportunity!

4.10 Employee Benefits regulations:

To achieve right amount of social justice , government from time to time create work rules or suggest modified guidelines to carry out work in regulatory environment ! Provision of provident funds, mediclaim , health insurance , safe working conditions, PPE, weekly work hours , minimum wages , shift timings and mandatory holidays , leave structure and its availability , extra work compensation and gender proportion for certain roles ! All such kind of regulations keep coming when a particular society need get developed and which is then governed by following relevant law of the land! In recent COVID-19 outburst, government regularly provided guidelines to business houses about working hours and people safety to stop infection spreading!

4.11 Duties & Tax Regulations:

Business and government has very very close relation with each other as far as tax changes are concerned! Taxes are mandatory and they have to paid on time to avoid sudden raids and penalty! Penalty is often hefty and one can easily pay the tax as soon as any financial transaction is taking place! You don't have to keep extra time for same! Hence as a good business owner, you have to pay relevant government taxes and ensure you procure and export material with adhering to it's right tax liability! ⊛⊛⊛

CHAPTER 5: BUSINESS CAPITAL

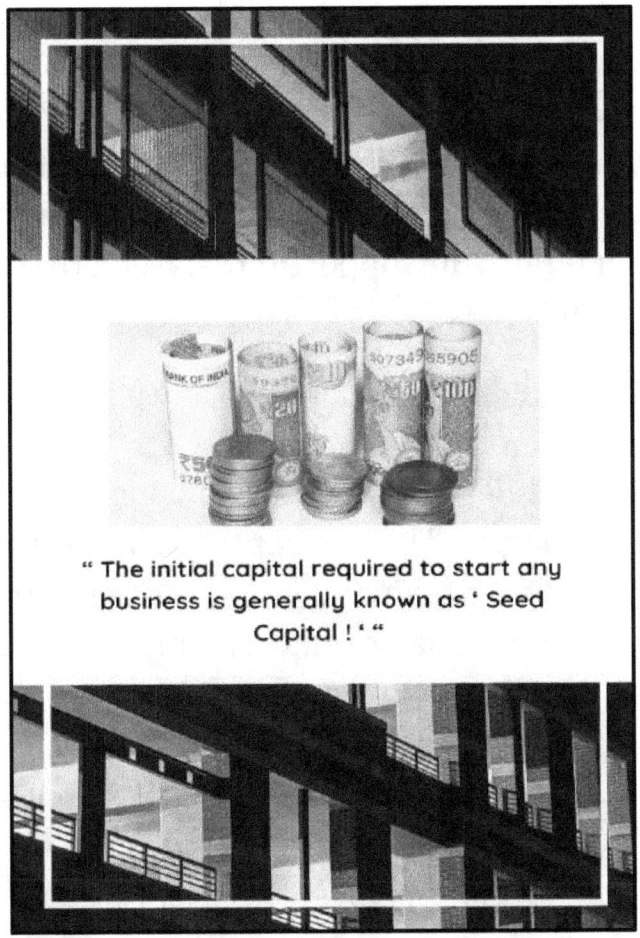

" The initial capital required to start any business is generally known as ' Seed Capital ! ' "

Image Courtesy : Rupixen , Unsplash.com

5.1 Introduction:

Hello Friends,

In this chapter, we are going to see one of the most important fluids of any business activity, which is known as business capital! The importance of business capital will be elaborated with respect to different applications of business capital through practical business needs! So let's enumerate the opportunities, where business capital is must!

1) Seed Capital :

While starting any business you need money! This is simple five letter word but it has its own role in business structure! The initial capital required to start any business is generally known as ' Seed Capital ' as although it is small in amount , later on as business progresses , it goes on increasing by adding profits from just started business activity ! People start their business through small business capital as small as ten lakhs to ten crores!

It depends upon the basic business size and number of people employed there!

2) <u>Working Capital :</u>

While performing daily business activities, you need instant money to pay bills and advances! The part of total capital which is available for these day to day or monthly financial activities is known as working capital!

Organizations have to ensure optimum level of working capital to ensure proper liquidity in major business transactions! You can put certain financial limits up to which financial transactions can be done and beyond which they are transferred to different helpdesk where large fund value is handled by business leaders depending upon necessity of that financial transaction at that time !

So, if you want to purchase 100 Kg Mild steel bar with suppose average price as 70 Rs/Kg and if bill is coming around 7500-8000 Rs adding various taxes and transportation values, that bill can be authorized by respective purchase manager with final approval of chief of business operations! However when you want to stock 50 Metric tons of mild steel bars with its rate 65 Rs per Kg , the total bill amounting between 33 Lakhs-35 Lakhs need to be approved by special authorities considering overall steel price forecast of that particular quarter or semester or complete year ! Here, if after purchasing such bulk stock, prices are going to be decreased by 5 Rs per Kg, you will receive costly material till order stock lasts and on each purchase; you have to encounter loss of 5 Rs per Kg! So if 50 Tons material is there, you will encounter loss of 2.5 Lakhs for that year!

If you consider other aspect in which steel become costlier by 10 Rs for whole year, you are going to receive the material at 10 Rs cheaper as per your trade contract! You will get saving of 5 Lakhs per annum because of your business decision! So, to think rationally about purchase decisions, you must have strong know how of major purchases and their as on today status and expected future forecast! Market analyst predicts the anticipated price rise or price drop regularly through their market review study! Based on monthly requirement collected from material and order planning function, you decide the plan of purchases and accordingly you approve bills of higher value!

Again to meet the needs of higher purchases you have to make arrangement of funds as per your contract terms! If purchaser gives you condition that at least 30% advance to be paid before purchase and rest 70% after sixty days , then you have to disburse advance against order and when you receive money from your customers after serving them through your products , the remaining 70% to be paid to purchaser ! This makes your purchase deal complete and trustworthy!

Once you repeat such transactions regularly, your credit at purchaser end increases and in future, he or she may allow you to purchase more material so that your business needs can be fulfilled!

This is what actual business relation is! Everyone is linked to other! More purchase at sells end means he also has great business opportunity and more purchase as producers end means, he has more orders in hand! So, if business has to prosper, both seller and purchaser must follow some basic business philosophy which is based on mutual co-operation and order clarity! If you have some huge material requirement, you have to communicate to your seller in advance which will be verified to district level stockiest or group of stockiest with the help of which same can be fulfilled at agreed price! If you have material requirement which cannot be fulfilled by any stockiest, then you have to contact raw material manufacturers for that order so that they will manufacture for you and will provide directly from company! If your requirement is so huge that it may not be fulfilled by domestic producers, then you have to search export market of different countries! Some countries have monopoly of some standard raw material supply!

You have to contact them and ask for rock bottom price! Based on your requirement, regular purchase and overall trade relation which involve foreign currency exchange values, you may be given a long term lasting business deal! Thus you can purchase required material by modifying your order details!

3) <u>Major Capital :</u>

Important business decisions are taken based on your major capital in the business! This capital can be in the form of reserves and surplus aggregated over the years in the business, this capital can be in the form of your savings in the bank which can be realized when you need it for your business, this can be in the form of your assets, which can be sold partially or fully to make way for a business solution! Suppose , you have a nonfunctioning business facility created fifty years ago and now the area is declared as residential zone , then in such condition , you can always auction that property and get its right value by sales ! So, this money on selling nonfunctioning asset becomes your capital! Later, you can purchase demarked plots for your business expansion in some other region, other state or other country! Because of such instantly available business capital, your business decisions become faster and you get the necessary momentum!

4) Equity Capital :

Business when grows and become public, promoters issues shares for purchase and business capital is raised! However in this form of capital, you have to give returns to investors in the form of dividends and you also have to ensure, you perform well in the market and keep earning regular profits! So, if you are not able to deliver good products that meet customer needs, your share prices will not grow as you will get less traffic of investors, however if your business shown aggressive plans and results, more people will try to purchase your stakes and hence because of rise in demand and better performance your stock values will go on increasing!

Many businesses, before raising equity capital decide about how many shares they will make available in open trading market! The stake proportion indicates the business independence! If you need more money from market, you have to leave shares from your basket and thus you may lose the major control of business from your hand!

Later on, when business is not performing well or share prices keep falling, people will sell shares of your company to get their money back and hence thus you own a strict liability to return the invested money in the form of shares! So if the capacity of returning stakeholders money is not available, you may go bankrupt and hence may face legal enquiries and associated market penalties for not being faithful towards shareholders interest! In your annual general meetings, you will be questioned by shareholders about your business decisions and hence you will be always answerable to public for your firm's performance! So, clever businesses rely of creating a mammoth business capital from where they can meet their financial needs and they keep inventing in their product offering so that they can book good profit with regular business development which will assist further expansion in different business verticals!

5) Securities :

Securities are funds which assures business existence! Before making any business deal, other parties may ask to keep some security amount with them so that in case of any unexpected business outcome they can recover anticipated business losses! Such fund is made available either through financial channels or through business resources!

Financial channels are nothing but banks and investment agencies which make necessary funds available for you at predetermined interest! When you receive such fund, you can do financial transactions and later when you receive funds from your own business activities you can pay the balance amount which is due and can regain security amount! Security amount can be again repaid to financial channels from where you raised this capital!

So, financial channels trust you based on your business credentials and you perform business with customer as per their requirement so that you get the required price! The part of the accumulated funds from business activity is paid as principle and interest for financial channels contribution to business and retained part can be used for business expansions!

The financial channels can provide these funds for long term or short term! FII – Foreign institutional investment and FDI- Foreign direct investment can provide you these funds till your business get started and later they can get expected returns on their investments! In future if business keep performing well, percentage of investment may increase!

6) Emergency or Contingency Funds or Capital :

Some business situations require huge fund approval in shortest possible time! Part of the funds made available for such urgencies is known as emergency or contingency funds! Basically, only supreme business leader can approve this fund! Before such approvals, the urgency is deeply studied and fund requirement is assessed, if the emergency fund is available completely, same is approved! If fund is lesser, alternative arrangement is required to meet the quick business need which can be fulfilled by either checking at financial channels or by selling non-performing assets!

You can always move out from business by selling your business! The interested businesses through various corporate strategies of merger, acquisition, and tie up may purchase your business and can make an attractive deal!

Business capital has its importance till you are performing business!

So, business capital is ultimate business need and without the help of which business sustainability become difficult! Now we can understand the effects of economic downturns on business functions and economic boom on business outcome!

When we study economics deeply, we clearly understand the need of maintaining equilibrium between demand and supply as well as features of macroeconomics and micro economics!

A successful businessman knows his business priorities and his business relaxations! Accordingly team of professionals decides the functioning of various business systems and their interdependence!

So, when you are becoming a businessman, you have to ensure a critical quality defect is not consuming your raw material more than 10% extra else you will encounter loss on additional material usage!

When you are consuming energy, you have to ensure, certified energy audits are carried out to ascertain the energy consumption and hence its financial implications! Several units of energy consumed extra put a financial pressure of several lakhs for your annual energy requirement!

When you are setting up a purchase cycle for raw material purchase, you have to ensure you are regularly paying up advances and remaining bills so that there will be no shortage in material supply! Before manufacturing stage get ready, you have to arrange material for consumption!

Once, we study all such ground level aspects of business, then we clearly understand the need of business capital and accordingly we learn to manage the need of business capital! Business capital is precious business entity! One has to take its care thoroughly! ✳✳✳

CHAPTER 6: EXPECTED MARKETS

"Domestic markets hold the major responsibility of meeting domestic need of small to huge population!"

Image Courtesy: Somi Jaiswal , Unsplash.com

6.1 Introduction:

Hello Friends,

In this chapter, we are going to see which are the types of various markets which every businessman is deeply interested for their growth and expansion as well as daily dealings of products and services! This insight will give us clear clarity about how business has to be done!

6.2 Nascent Market:

The early phase of product introduction or product launch is done with nascent market! Here, your product is offered to select and specific people who have highest possibility of its purchase! Off course, such products have special features and more applications compared to general products! Journey of nascent market starts with know-how of new product! Since people are accustomed to regular products, many people prefer not to change with new one! Here, as you present advantages of new product over regular product, people start using new product with small sample purchase! If the results are satisfactory, they give regular orders and thus nascent market get developed over period of time! With its development, more and more players get added and monopoly of any one producer gets appropriated! The early bird benefit is achieved by inventor and later on they keep reinventing new products so that they can keep an edge over their competitors!

6.3 Domestic Market:

Domestic market is the marketplace inside the country where product is manufactured! Basically, the place of manufacturing get labeled on manufactured product as 'Made in India ', 'Made in USA', 'Made in UK'!

The national boundaries inside which manufactured product get its sales is known as domestic market! Domestic market composed of different layers! You have state market, interstate market, district market, inter district market, taluka market- inter taluka market, village market- inter village market! City- village market, City – districts market, etc.! The manufactured good keep moving throughout your country and applicable taxes are levied on its purchase and sales!

Domestic markets hold the major responsibility of meeting domestic need of small to huge population! In country like India where national population is around one thirty crores, scope of development of domestic market is huge and once you know the market requirements, your sales get started as soon as you deliver your product!

6.4 International or Export Market:

Manufactured products or services which meet needs of foreign nationals through a dedicated market are known as Export Market! Here trade of product and services is done from one nation to another nation! Numbers of regulations are followed before sending material to final customer! Before making a purchase decision, requirements of products are communicated and if products meets requirement, then they are accepted!

Every nation has certain resources and certain scarcity! Resources which are abundance in availability are traded to different countries through official trading route and resources which are scarce are purchased from other country, also following official trade route!

The important aspect of any export business is its legitimate functioning! You have to follow strict business regulations, code of ethics and integrity, financial transparency, product quality, duties and taxes payment, mutual co-operation in area of influence, after sales service and reporting! If you are able to handle the overseas market, then you can achieve multifold growth in sufficient time frame!

Companies book huge profits serving export customer and clients! This is because, you get chance to serve because of your talent and economical availability! The rewards or remuneration you received get multifold value in your nation if your currency is depreciating than export currency! Export market has unique benefits and international reach!

6.5 Remote Market:

A clever businessman always tries to focus on remote market! This is because; the competition is comparatively less as more players avoid reaching such markets just because of long lead times and comparatively easy markets are available nearby!

The fundamental provision of infrastructure is not available in such market and if you manage all by yourself, you can get regular chance of serving such market!

E.g. If you want to sell your newly launched solar energy products to a remote region where sunlight is available in abundance throughout the year, what you do, you manufacture the products where the relevant ecosystem is present and you create a trade route or dealers channel where these products can be easily sold through proper marketing, advertising and promoting to desired customers! This is how remote markets are reached from place of its manufacturing!

Now remote market can be domestic or international! When computer was invented, it was exported to various countries because production was limited to few nations, later as demand keep growing and technology become accessible, manufacturing started from various locations and international requirement is fulfilled! So, over the period of time, this remote market gets converted into domestic market! Markets experience such changes as the product gets its sales volume! Local manufacturing facilities are developed which can meet the local need of international products! If you have a standard manufacturing, design and commissioning process, you can carry out work in any country adhering to their local laws of the land! This makes business extremely simplified and truly global!

6.6 Untapped Market:

This is open market! No one knows about your product and you have created a wonderful product which is highly useful for society and you are about to launch this product internationally! You will never imagine the size of untapped market! It's very very huge!

E.g. when smartphones just introduced internationally, within few months millions users switched to smartphone from their earlier handsets! When LED TV's are introduced in the market, billion users switched to LED over earlier CRT screen! When small budget SUV's are introduced in the market, many people bought their own dream car and preferred to travel on their own! So, the market available to manufacturers was huge and extremely huge! Many investors invested promising amount in developing new ventures and keep supplying these products from these regions regularly! People are estimating that even shops are running 24 x 7 , the demand is not going to fulfill till next five or ten years ! This is what known as untapped market! You have extremely high level of demand for your innovative product! So, as a businessman, the most important thing one has to focus is finding a technical solution that transforms people's daily living experience! When people find it useful, they get switched to new product or service! Benefit of untapped market is to be taken before more service providers like you come there, serve there!

6.6 Digital Market:

We have seen various markets and their potential, with recent development in computer and information technology along with innovations in telecommunication, digital space is recognized as new market which is accessible to anyone with the power of internet! Era of digitalization is extremely important factor of universal market dynamics!

Now establishments can do major activities and minor activities with the help of online platforms! Advanced computer systems are capable of handling big business data; they can transfer this data wherever there is connection!

On a click of the mouse , now you can review all company details , their vision , mission , policies , manpower capacity , skills in the organization , projects delivered, awards won , certifications received and accordingly you can place required orders ! Even all financial transactions also can be done digitally! This way of doing business is global and now procurement and supply of various parts become very much easy!

6.7 Space Market:

Although, this market is very very niche and yet not developed, it is not nascent nor remote, it is available in space universe!

Science is doing great progress and many companies are now involved to find out an opportunity to live a life on different planet other than earth!

Again this market is in research and development stage and major dealings of such businesses happen through defined parameters and following strict confidentiality!

Satellite launch, Space shuttles, Astronaut Requirements, Digital telescopes and special lenses, possibility to have home in other planet etc. are being tried out!

In future markets, space market will be an important aspect of special businesses and prominent organizations will tap the opportunities as the progress is made!

Constant quest of market is identity of real businessman! This quest is inspiration behind business development! ✳✳✳

CHAPTER 7: BUSINESS INFLUENCE AND IMAGE

Image Courtesy : Steve Gale , Unsplash.com

7.1 Introduction:

Hello Friends,

In this chapter, we are going to see important aspects of influence of the business and image of the business as far as corporate governance is concerned!

7.2 How Business Influence Works:

Business is creative and productive activity! Every businessman always tries to provide a simple solution to complex problems through use of technology and genius! Technical products have long lasting impact on the minds of the customer! Every technical product meets a business need!

When transportation was being developed, two stroke engines, four stroke engines got developed! Later on various types of automobile designs are developed! Engine performance and speed limits along with mileage enhancement become regular activity of innovation! Every feature of developed automobile attracted customer and made experience of commuting easy! According to different price variations, new designs made buying automobile more easy! This influenced customer to look for various alternatives available at that time!

Now, as customers started using products, they noted actual performance and recommended each other to go for it! This improved popularity of the product and later on manufacturing company also presented image of the business as something very very special for the customers! This business image is subsequently enlarged with new business campaigns and development of new product!

Ability to connect developed product to emotional and practical need of customer become one of the important aspect of product development! Company image is highly dependent of product quality and product service! So, as customer started receiving various products and their service, company image is deeply identified by the customer into their mind! This image helped new products to launch easily and get required sales through exact advertisement and promotions!

7.3 Exact Role of Corporate Governance in building business image and business influence:

Corporate Governance has following key functions to build business image –

a) When things are planned at corporate level, they have clear thoughts and action plans about what kind of products or services they want to offer to their target customers! The type of setting helps to design the products accordingly with the help of designers and later same are delivered to customers through manufacturing capability!

b) Another important aspect of development of business influence is gaining the required equity capital necessary for the business operations! Business influence has great effect on developing and maintaining the business capital through equity! It is observed that when an organization starts growing, prices of its shares go on increasing! When same organization expands in different nations, its shares start growing, this is clear indication of business influence! As business keep growing and performing well, its positive influence affects customer perception which gets converted into his willingness to invest and buy the shares!

c) When the organization takes some strategic decisions like increasing head count, providing salary hikes, making loans available for financial needs through organizations welfare fund, it improves level of business influence! More people feel positive about the business development and efficiency also get improved! This results into building good level of business image also!

d) Business influence keeps changing! When the company is performing well, your influence is positive as business gets highlighted in various trade shows, exhibitions, product seminars, new product launch! When the business is not performing well due to loss making, less orders, customer satisfaction concerns, business influence get reduced! So, as a good practice of corporate governance, business image need to be keep intact so as business influence remains there for long time in market dynamics!

e) When sudden recessions or business boom occurs, the effect of positive business influence helps businesses to grow! In recessions, although you have less business opportunities in recent time but because of your past performance, business houses keep constant trust on your ability and keep investing or giving orders however small they are! In times of recession, meeting break – even point of the business and being in the business is more important! When the state of recession slowly go away and business opportunities start growing , because of maintained business influence , customer pour new orders and thus business momentum get an instant rise ! Business image maintained in difficult business time get its due credit and which get reflected into enhanced business opportunities! Each passing year, when this habit is maintained, business becomes more stable and prosperous!

7.4) Types of Business Images:

To understand business in more simple form, let's see types of business images here!

a) **Solution Provider**: Businesses are specialist of business solution! When more complex problems are solved by businesses in long term, their image come to know as solution provider!

b) **Market Leaders**: Few businesses always stay ahead and create new solution before someone enters there! Doing this practice for many years, image of the business come to known as market leader!

c) **Low cost producers**: Some products are required in abundance and few businesses got expertise in developing them in low cost keeping required quality level intact!

d) **Environment Friendly**: This is very much important business image in current scenario! The products which you create need to be less harmful to your environment! More environment friendly products you create, more people prefer to procure these products!

e) **Future ready**: Some organizations always create products which are very much new and no one has attempted to create them earlier! Through their dedicated research and development, they develop future markets and slowly pitch their new products in the league!

f) **Complete Package**: Leading organizations provide turnkey solutions to various customers as per their different needs! If you purchase such products, the chances of looking for different alternatives become very less, because in one product basket, you get almost everything you needed! Such organizations develop their identity as complete package provider! ✳✳✳

CHAPTER 8 : CUSTOMER CARE

" The design of supporting services is made in such a way that important needs of customer can be addressed easily! "

Image Courtesy:Kelly Sikkema , Unsplash.com

8.1 Introduction:

Hello Friends,

In this chapter, we are going to see some specific points about customer care which are important when corporate governance is concerned! Through these points, relation between trade and profit will be understood easily!

8.2 Product Care:

Image Courtesy:Giorgio Trovato, Unsplash.com

Every product is genuine creation from manufacturer's side. Every manufacturer takes care that final product meets the requirements mentioned while initiating orders. When work is in process, some additional requirements also get included which are incorporated through authorized change notes! This end to end communication indicates the degree of customer care and fulfillment of ad-hoc queries and questions! As far as corporate governance is concerned , you have to make a system in place where all customer requirements can be easily channelized to different routes like marketing , design , purchase, quality , manufacturing , servicing , projects ,warehouse so that everyone knows their scope and its fulfillment within time limit!

8.3 Pricing Care:

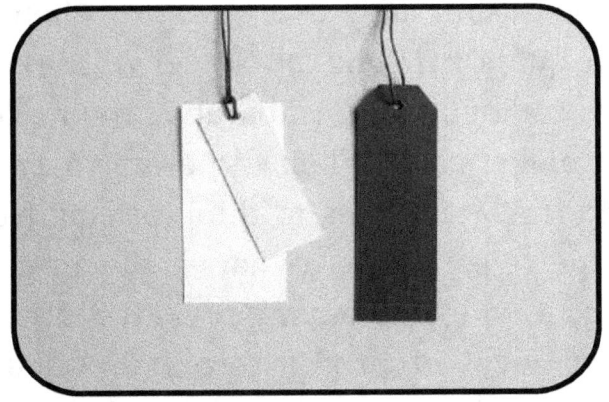

Image Courtesy:Angele Kamp , Unsplash.com

Every manufacturer has to take care of this aspect of product or service delivery where they have to ensure right price is attached to their products! Price is always a good balance between how much profit expected as manufacturer and how much amount customer will ready to pay without a second thought! Manufacturers put their hard efforts on improving processes so that cost will be minimum and a good price can be worked out without much hesitation on profit compromise! The quantity factor also plays an important role when we are taking care of deciding price! Cost of production get reduced when bulk quantity is manufactured which can allow to keep price low! Less quantity you manufacture in a roll , you have to again set resources in next roll which again adds increased service costs , hence more is the quantity in one roll , lesser will be costs and price can be lower comparative to one received with higher cost ! When corporate governance is concerned, team has to think pricing from two perspectives – One- What is the price of my product which meets my break-even point and sound level of profit! Second – What is my competitor's price and if I keep it lesser or more

what will be effect on product sales and overall
turnaround!

8.4 Servicing Care:

Image Courtesy:Eric Mclean, Unsplash.com

Every customer needs a dedicated service when
the product is actually sold! This service can be
quick installation service, commissioning
support, inter processing validation support,
scheduled inspection support, replacement
services support, maintenance services support!
The design of supporting services is made in
such a way that important needs of customer can
be addressed easily!

You have purchased a new product and after one month of its purchase, a small defect is noticed. Then after communication to customer care representative how fast the service get active is the degree of customer care available with that product! Very high level of service standards improves business influence and business image! Rather instant customer service is backbone of earning descent profits!

Now days, we have automated chat bots for taking care of customer service. You have dedicated service segments and customer has to choose one in which he needs your support. With selected option, set algorhythem follows the necessary service path and authorized representative helps or pre-determined service solution is executed!

As technology will keep improving, better service standards will be evolved! With digital revolution, now providing rating to received service is become very simple! Because of rating and feedback, people easily come to know about the product quality and practical experience of people who used your products!

8.5 Packaging Care:

Image Courtesy:Leone Venter, Unsplash.com

This is again one of the important points when customer care is concerned! Packaging of product is very much important when product transportation is critical aspect! When material is procured from overseas market, you need to ship that material through seaworthy packaging! The traveling time can be around fifteen days to one month or may be more! In that time frame, your material should not corrode! You have to take care of packaging in such a way that main part is covered in appropriate wrapping material denoted in its packing guide and same is maintained for related other components !

8.6 In process Manufacturing Care:

Image Courtesy: Rafael Juarez , Unsplash.com

Often it is regarded as good practice to show the flow of actual product processing when it is happening in process! You may invite customer to visit your facility for one or two critical stage inspection so that before dispatching he can provide remark and comments about product quality or overall completeness! If customer suggests one or two improvement points other than system manual, manufacturer will also assess the need and will try to fulfill the requirement! Corporate governance is not only about financial discipline it's about customer care in every segment of business with equal zeal and professionalism! ✸✸✸

CHAPTER 9 : INNOVATION

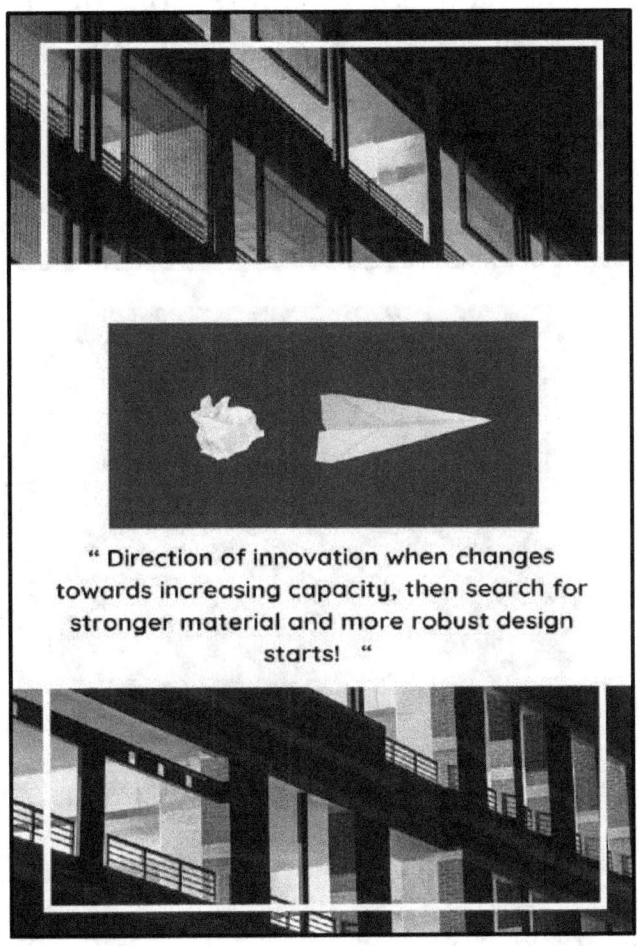

" Direction of innovation when changes towards increasing capacity, then search for stronger material and more robust design starts! "

Image Courtesy: Mat Ridley , Unsplash.com

9.1 Introduction:

Hello Friends,

This chapter of corporate governance deals with concept of innovation and its long term effect on business sustenance which is major aspect of governance of any kind!

9.2 Base of Long term Corporate Governance:

Image Courtesy: Tim Hufner, Unsplash.com

When we consider concept of business, its long term activity! Everyone wishes that the machine of providing service to customer must run constantly! Business as a basic plan is considered as long term proposition of supplying new products which meet daily needs! Every product has certain shelf life! In corporate sector, people keep inventing new models which are better or different than previous model! Continuous research in scientific direction allows new innovations to happen that caters customers need!

When governance is in place, it tries to serve the customer through systematic arrangement of resources and business capital! Good way of governance involves anticipating requirements of customers in advance, tackling technological challenges along with and surpass those challenges and then through accurate process of product creation to distribution, supply the readymade products!

First year of business is always a learning year where you actually goes through system application for initiating customer service! In second year, when same cycle gets repeated, you are more certain about all dealings need to be done! The further year is still easy! Because having experience of three years helps you to prioritize annual business plan, adjust to changes in demands which happens through year with respect to collected data and later fine tune the demand-supply equation! Once you are near to five year plan you get clear idea of doing the business and by this time your capital is also increased to sufficient level at which business transactions can be done easily! But what if, business didn't run for three years and beyond and get stucked in between?

When business is started with initial orders, till the order completion and receiving customer feedback, you have to track all details happening at customer end! You need to take feedback about how the product is functioning, if there are any problems during operation, how product can be made better! Such feedbacks adds to knowledge base of business and by making those changes in business modeling , product keep improving and it helps to increase business in coming years !

When more and more people start using your product, your customers reach increases and thus business gets its required momentum! Even though if sometime demand is decreased or complaints are received, you have to immediately look for resolving them! This approach helps you to take care of the business!

9.3 Contribution of Corporate Governance in boosting speed of innovation:

Deciding the ultimate extent of business capital which has to be invested in innovation is a strategic decision! Suppose 15% of profit is invested in research and development activity for an annual investment! Then number of scientist or project leaders will start research on concepts which are completely new, few concepts which are next step of current research and few concepts which can increase portability of products!

Innovation is always focused with which we can reduce weight of final product so that less material will be consumed, research can be done on reducing density by use of alternative material, for temperature control another thermostatic material can be researched which has less heat dissipation factor, so direction of innovation is always towards making products more simpler and more compact!

Direction of innovation when changes towards increasing capacity, then search for stronger material and more robust design starts! Design of high capacity products need to have excellent safety features because in unexpected incidences, the loss to the property and people is very much severe than product with less capacity!

Direction of innovation when shift towards finding a unique solution or new solution, the emerging technologies are used! Research in such area is in early stage of its development and when your firm gets that research completed, the product created get good response from market which helps business to prosper!

The moment of getting the required breakthrough is always special and specific in innovation! When our study on project is going on, we get some hints about new findings. When important clues are found further searching in that direction give us more inputs and later we get full-fledged picture of scientific property! Then we apply techno commercial thinking to convert the observed property into a sound technical solution! Because of commercial viability, solution implementation in huge scale become possible and through every sales, profit from business keep improving as month and year in the business keeps growing!

So based on the need of the market as well as recent development in technology, corporate governance decides the level of interest which is necessary to invest in innovative research work!

9.4 Effects of not focusing on innovations:

Any business is best example of selling new research through development of creative product! Science shows the way of materialistic progress and technology actually builds that way! So, as per your vision, you get the path of your business progress!

There is certain time frame till which newly developed product remains in demand! When the demand is lost, the sales get reduced! So, as a clever businessman, you have to keep your product basket ready which will keep your business demand in tact! Business owners or professional engaged in business development if forget to provide required attention in innovation, they may have to face issues in demand creation! Product demand is first and last step of business progress!

Few companies create typical products over years and still remain in the business for several years! Suppose a tyre company uses the same material for its production and can provide you hundred odd varieties of tyres of different sizes, configurations and price range! Tyre being the item of regular demand for automobile sector, the manufacturer remains in the business for long time even though there are more competitors!

In another example , other business owner develops only four to five varieties and he also remain in business for same no of years but his growth is limited than the earlier manufacturer ! This is because , first business owner invest part of his profit in developing hundred different products in various capacities and design and hence provide more options to customer ! That is the reason, he is able to serve more customers and hence get more business! Business is simple when efforts are directed towards innovation! Corporate Governance supports innovation!
⊛⊛⊛

CHAPTER 10 : DESIGN & DIGITALIZATION

" Digitally now design can be copied, saved, edited, modified, transported, compressed, can be coded, can be encrypted! "

Image Courtesy: Domenico Loia , Unsplash.com

10.1 Introduction:

Hello Friends,

In this chapter, we are going to see how the product design, process design, system design affects the energy inside corporate governance! The vibrant corporate governance is nothing but cumulative effect of product design, process design and system design! Design is considered as soul of the business! The firm having productive and sturdy design is always ahead of their competitors! Let's see into the details!

<u>10.2 Features of Product Design:</u>

Image Courtesy: Kumpan Electric , Unsplash.com

i) Design of product is ultimate identity of firms manufacturing capability and solution oriented approach of business!

ii) Better designs makes process setting easy which in turn takes less time for product realization and hence provide better throughput in available production hours!

iii) Repeatability of the design and overall accommodativeness is guiding factor when productive designs are created! Your design must provide complete usage of available resources so that very less scrap is generated and good amount of material is used!

iv) Digitalization of design makes a safer design! Here, you can cross check whether designed model is safe with respect to its overall structure, specifications and portability! Virtual performance of product design indicates parameters that will boost efficiency and parameters which needs right kind of control when product experience out of tolerance situations! Unless we model the product in virtual show, we can't design an accurate design. Because of simulations, we are able to understand the actual functioning of the product when it is created physically!

v) Digitally now design can be copied, saved, edited, modified, transported, compressed, can be coded, can be encrypted! As far as design data security is required, digital usage has enhanced overall status of security! Digital application helps designers to get their work done in least amount of time!

vi) Earlier drafting a drawing when design is made was a Hercules's task! Draftsman used to spend lots of time manually to design templates and draw various views on drawing paper which was then provided for manufacturing! As soon as Xerox machines are arrived, design copies become possible! So drafting single drawing and then distributing same to various departments become possible! When computers arrived, creating drawing becomes extremely convenient. Now you can try different combinations and you don't have to draw the drawing again and again! You simply can modify the portion where change is required or you can create new file and later you can draw new part on that drawing! Drafting software's provided 3D view of the object and hence minute detailing become easy! More detail is the drawing, better is the functionality of the part! Sometime what happen, when a part is fitted to other part through threads and nut combination, their assembly become weak! This is unsafe condition and when part is in operation, it can result into accident or injury because of loose connection! When we note the root cause, we observe the given thread combination of male and female part side is not done of required pitch because of which there is mismatch and loose connection! Hence while designing, we have to take care of mating parts so that they don't foul with each other, they don't intersect each other, and they don't block each other's path!

vii) Digitally empowered designs can encounter various revisions as part gets developed! These changes are always updated in drawing schedule so that track of all changes can be maintained!

viii) Product design and its control is internal soul of corporate governance! One design can create million parts which can be sold to million customers worldwide! So, corporate governance gives keen eye to developments related to product design! Most of the time, it is observed that person heading the organization has sound experience of designing world class products in past because of which he can sell the ultimate customer solution!

10.3 Features of Process Design:

Image Courtesy : Martin Adams , Unsplash.com

When product design is finalized, one has to also think on parallel path about process design! Your product may involve various shapes, their sizes, their manufacturing operations and material trimming procedures! Accordingly your processes must support that product design. It means when you are planning for a rolling operation in product design, you must know the maximum capacity of rolling machine inside the plant or which can be done from outside! If rolling capacity is lesser then you have to break the part into two parts which can be rolled and joined together!

Similarly, product design must ensure that processes can be carried out flexibly! So that in same design, you can do part cutting, you can weld that part, you can paint that part and you can assemble that part! More and more flexibility is available in design, better work can be sequenced and there will be less need to wait for other parts as process can be continued independently of each other!

In right type of process design, the next process is the system of checks and balances of earlier process! In smart process design, intermediate stage gets accepted only when it's all parameters are satisfactory! Design of the process in the form of jigs and fixtures is done in such a way that , if allowable tolerance is not maintained , then part will not get fitted in next process set up because of which you have to correct the earlier step and then you can go ahead for next process step !

Suppose, if this no go zone of process design is not available and if process fixture accept the part as it is, then part will move with error and later it will get stuck in the middle causing some sort of major trouble for the product being manufactured!

Another important aspect of efficient process design is its seamlessness! When product completes one stage, it needs to be moved to next stage! When it completes the second stage, it needs to be moved to third stage! Similarly the flow of material must follow the desired path with which product get its final shape and size!

In smart process design, the waste generated in the process workout is collected through dedicated collectors placed in nearby zone! Every process waste is useful especially if you are working with metal parts! The cut parts can be sold as scrap of various grades and hence overall costing of the process can be minimized! Process waste can be collected at the end of each step or they can be stocked in dedicated area through connecting pipeline!

The study of waste material is prime concern of material department which keep tally of material stock and its consumption! If material consumption shows the difference, then process waste cannot be calculated accurately and hence valuable material get wasted without a record! This adds to direct losses to business and hence collection of major process waste which can be sold again is essential!

10.4 Features of System Design:

Image Courtesy :Kelly Sikkema , Unsplash.com

Corporate governance is about better systems and its elaborative design! A system is major functional requirement which drives business momentum! A fast paced system communication ensures everyone in the system and related to system get the necessary message on business development and they can perform their job! A loose or weak system design indicates lethargy and slowness in the operations! The business strategies in such systems are lengthy and they require many approvals which make business environment having lots of compulsion and less degree of freedom!

Hence as a better corporate governance designer, you have to take care of your system in such a way that your product design is simplest to understand to every functional unit which can save time of communication, your process design must be so easy and accurate that system of checks and balances is available in next step and your flow of decisions has to be quick and correct! With digital advantage system integration with product design and process design become easy! ✷✷✷

CHAPTER 11 : RAW MATERIAL PROCUREMENT

" Every businessman has a wish to procure raw material from genuine suppliers! "

Image Courtesy: Shail Sharma , Unsplash.com

11.1 Introduction:

Hello Friends,

In this chapter, we are going to see important aspects of raw material procurement through corporate governance perspective! Raw material is major consumable of entire business activities and hence its meticulous planning and implementation is ideal way of progressing in business!

11.2 Types of Raw Material:

Every business needs raw material! Raw material is the input which is processed to give certain desirable output! In metal industries, raw material can be minerals, metal composites, metal ores, metal remains! In processing industries dealing with metallic parts, metal ingots and raw castings can be raw material! In fabrication industries raw material can be plates, tubes, pipes, bars which are cut and fitted either by welding or riveting or by any other joining process!

When we consider oil and gas industries, raw material is crude oil which is to be refined in the form of various products! In software industries, raw material can be programming input or language code which is transformed to generate necessary system output software! In mobile applications the operating system supports applications in such a way that when right type of input is entered, the co-related output will be shown which is already feed in the system through mathematical formulae in the form of software code! It means, when you want to add two digits and find out its total, you will prepare an addition code where you will tell to input A & B which equals output C! Here basic mathematical formulae are readily available which are used by software! The internal IC's are equipped with different logic gates which give required outcomes! Various programming languages work as input while developing software which later derives a predefined output when given conditions are met! Number of software's is built by the computer genius after studying the mathematical and logical relation between various entities!

11.3 From Where to procure raw material?

This is again one of the million dollar question of corporate governance strategies! Every businessman has a wish to procure raw material from genuine suppliers! This is first and foremost important requirement and expectation! Secondly, the raw material needs to be regularly supplied when payment is made as per the contractual terms! Third part, the raw material need to be certified by authorized material inspection agencies so that we can rely on its physical and mechanical properties and even though we make bulk purchases ranging to several tons, the material quality must remain same in provided batch!

There are raw material manufacturers, steel mills, tube drawing facilities, foundries where raw material needed for metal industries is procured! Company may have authorized channel of material procurement which happens through distributor, dealer, local stockiest, retailer and vendors –traders link! The prices of material vary in all sales stations and they are determined by company! More is the purchase, less is the price and same can be negotiated to a certain level! Moreover, if the orders are fixed and certain, you may enter into rate contract terms and can get material up to certain credit limit by which you can process your work without any worry. You have to just communicate your requirement and get the needed material!

Rating of material supplier as well known material supplier, star rated material supplier, export quality material supplier, EN 3.1 or EN 3.2 classified material supplier is essential to widely know the quality of material being supplied! When financial terms of material supply are discussed, material can be procured with payment of advance and rest of the payment can be done within agreed credit limit! If the 100 % payment required before purchase, most of the time, material is procured at little bit discounted price!

Advantages of material procurement from genuine seller are endless as it reflects through your final product quality! The corporate governance thinking always develops way where trade is done with reputed material supplier so that brand image remains intact!

11.4 Frequency and Intervals of material procurement:

In annual system of financial accounting, many corporates focus on quarterly order flow! Basically, when quarterly requirement of orders is known, suppose a manufacturer has to supply 30 products in three months with average of 10 products per month, then for first month the material requirement will be calculated from the bills of material available in the drawing! The orders of different type of material are segregated separately and material suppliers are decided based on their prospectus or actual business meetings!

When enquiries are generated, material suppliers respond as per their price, stock and material certificate availability! Material procurement department negotiate with the suppliers as per the corporate procurement guidelines and instructions! Business developers are constantly in contact with influential market leaders who derive the equations of material purchase! Trade understandings and long term promises takes place between business developers by which they supply material at agreed price considering business growth aspects!

So you can order monthly material, quarterly material, half yearly stock material or annual requirement material! Based on the need of investing capital, material purchase is done to support lead time!

Corporates has to find out a middle way where material should not remain in inventory for longer time as idle material and material should be available just in time! These two factors decide the overall efficiency of the material procurement function!

Stocking policies are derived after noting the frequency of material required to carry out operations! Suppose in a steel mill where minerals are basic raw material, in such a case you have to take excess stock of minerals so that when mill is working with full capacity, material need to be available in right time! Any delay on material part will result into wastage of energy when mill is idle! This excess capacity , let's say 15% excess , 20 % excess is planned based on the experience of that months material demand !

11.5 Corporate Lobbies for raw material procurement and their market influence:

In business, raw material is bottleneck item! If raw material is not available, you can't precede your work! Also the price of the raw material is again a governing factor of business! When prices are low in the market, buying the material is quite affordable while when material prices are higher, you can't buy required quantity! Noting this basic thing, raw material suppliers and producers always interact with each other through their associations and organizations! They get the details of overall material creation in one year per annum in country , how much material is exported and how much material is consumed domestically, how the prices remained in the market and what are purchase trends !

Data is the base for influencing price in the material market! When you know a certain range of material demand, you can limit your production accordingly and hence can get price desired! Need of material procurement is seriously studied in the major aspects of Corporate Governance! ⊛⊛⊛

CHAPTER 12 :

MANUFACTURING PRACTICES

" Hence manufacturing is known as crown of the Corporate Governance! "

Image Courtesy: Gomi DS , Unsplash.com

12.1 Introduction:

Hello Friends,

In this chapter, we are going to see essence of corporate governance as experienced in manufacturing practices! It's such an interesting field of study which reflects the overall business commitment and its social usefulness!

12.2 Manufacturing is the crown of Corporate Governance:

When any type of system is analyzed for its smartness, usefulness, creativeness, the first and last thing handled is the products created by that system! If products show practical applications of all purposes for which it was created, then we can say that system is correct!

When governance is present inside a system, the power of governance actually facilitates system processes so that product gets created with right quality and right quantity! Quality is an important factor! If you are not producing quality adhering products, you will not able to sell them more than once or twice!

Third time or may be second time or in current scenarios, just mere by observing your products quality rating, the customer will rethink to make his purchase decision!

Secondly, quantity you produce is nothing but the simplest form of your productivity! More quantity you produce, more sales opportunities can be earned! Also, more quantity of production indicates your manufacturing system is capable of producing part having required features again and again!

So, when quality and quantity both are running the same path, governance at such system is observed to be more disciplined, productive and creative! These governance features ultimately create the brand image! When products manufactured under such style of corporate governance reach market, over the period of time, market get the feel of product performance and value for money proposition! When you purchase the product first time, second time, third time, your brand loyalty gets established! Which keep on going till you are interested in buying same product and till you don't get a better option !

Hence manufacturing is known as crown of the Corporate Governance! As crown is always observed on king's head and it is stable and beautiful, same ways, the products you supply in the market are representative of your self-esteem and production capability! A fancy and decorated crown with suitable strength has longer shelf life! For number of years, king likes to wear that crown! King never thinks of changing that crown as that crown has given a certain identity in the market!

Crown is worn in the meetings and on the war-field to indicate the influence of a king! Depending on the talent and capability, crown can be designed in different way! Similarly, depending on company sizes and investments, company can be called as small capital, medium capital, and large capital companies!

The growth of companies happens in systematic way! You have to meet the performance bands with which you can be known as small cap, medium cap or large cap companies!

12.3 Recommended Manufacturing practices for reflecting true image of Corporate Governance:

Every organization is group of qualified, trained and resourceful people! People in the organization make wonders when they work either independently or in team! The talent available with them is utilized to create world class products and value adding services! Let's see elaborately, how manufacturing practices symbolize great corporate governance in place:

Image Courtesy: Clark Young , Unsplash.com

1) Good manufacturing practices starts with clear instructions to staff and operators with approved written procedure!

2) There is system manual in place which describes roles and responsibilities of every unit, every function and every person to deliver the given target effectively and efficiently!

3) Good manufacturing is about using right kind of material, following safe tools and tackles, ensuring cleanliness and order in work stations and giving required time to every operation till it reach its final outcome! You have to check final outcome by following its approved quality assurance plan! If the requirements in the quality plan are met, then you have to go ahead for next operation!

4) Manufacturing requires advanced machines and calibrated instruments! Firm's commitment to create quality product start with initial investment in machines and meteorology! Mind it; meteorology has its own significance in establishing your brand image and brand influence! Organization is known in business markets for the least count in which they regularly operate! The

organization capable of working in tolerances of micron get more precise work, more precious material to work with and hence better workmanship rates !

5) Skill of the organization is built because of good manufacturing practices! When you repeat good things over the years, it becomes your habit and good habit yield good outcome, good product and good service!

6) How much good one should behave in one organization is the million dollar question! The answer of this question lies in your ability to stretch your limits! Requirement of industry is huge, you can work round the clock to serve customers but in the end you get tired when you reach a certain level of performance! That's it, once you find the quality of your work is not getting proper result, you have to stop for a while, realign yourself to work and then start it after taking your time! The focus of good manufacturing lies in ability to create regular and consistent quality through technical approach!

7) In Corporate Governance, there is system of giving feedback to internal and external authorities through verbal and non-verbal communication! The aim of feedback is to give the idea about the product experience and service delivered! If feedback is good, you can continue with the process! If feedback is not good, then you have to work on the points which express the need of required correction!

8) Good manufacturing is about continuous development so that cycle time get reduce and system efficiency keep improving!

9) The skill of the organization manufacturing first unit as team and thousandth unit of the team goes through cycles of improvement projects, mistake proofing, alternating process parameters, studying experimental evaluations of technical improvements, and maintaining enhanced rigidity of work flow!

10) Corporate Governance is ownership! ⊛

CHAPTER 13 : SHIPPING AND COMMERCIAL

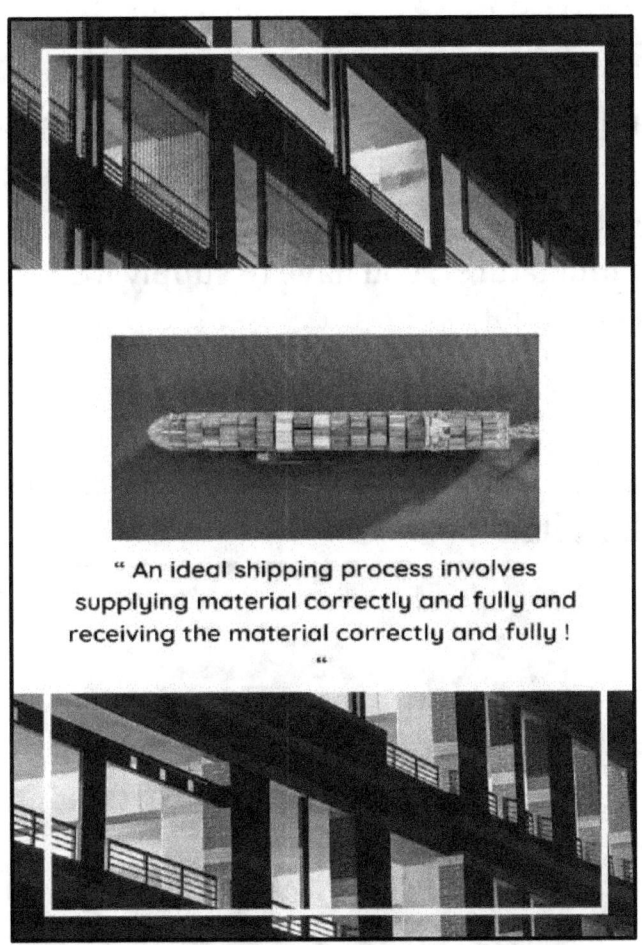

" An ideal shipping process involves supplying material correctly and fully and receiving the material correctly and fully ! "

Image Courtesy: Venti Views , Unsplash.com

13.1 Introduction:

Hello Friends,

In this chapter, we are going to see important aspects of most crucial final operation of internal business activity which is known as shipping and commercial! The hold of shipping and commercial activity is best indicator of Corporate Governance! Finish goods is customers ready to buy property and as a manufacturer, you have to supply it securely and accurately!

13.2 Ideal Corporate Governance for shipping:

Image Courtesy: Kira auf der , Unsplash.com

The role of shipping function come into play when your product is ready in all aspects and once the documentation of final clearance or final release is received , same can be packed and loaded on vehicle arrived to receive the product !

So, ideally, your product needs to be ready! It means, you must complete total design and manufacturing scope along with necessary testing and in-house certification of your products test performance! Its best engineering practice that every product and its critical intermediate stages need to be checked for its workmanship and accuracy by applying principles of quality assurance plan ! If quality principles are not respected with required degree, small or major defects get created inside the product which can cause unproductive and unsafe conditions at work . To avoid the same , manufacturers certification is must before product is dispatched from his or her premises !

Always remember , in corporate governance delay is acceptable but defect is not acceptable in final product !

During internal processing , stages are monitored and 'at actual observations' regarding product specifications are ascertained with respect to provided design details ! When a conformance is observed the clearance is given for going ahead ! When a non-conformance is observed , necessary NCR report is generated and which is acted upon for its required corrective actions and preventive actions ! Corrective actions correct defect observed in tested product while preventive action takes care that such defect is totally removed from system from occurring and necessary competence is built up to make people more knowledgeable about the defects cause and remedy of its removal !

So, a product ready for dispatch has completed stage inspection report , its material certificate and their identification details, test reports and various compliance report , if any external inspection agency is deputed for in process inspection then authorized release note from that agency about conformance to requirements , if few parts are purchased from outside the scope of manufacturer , then the manufacturers certificate of those parts , if any instruction manual is applicable then a copy of same need to be supplied with material being dispatched, separate packing list of consignment where different shipping boxes are available and material kept in that casing is labeled for easy identification ! The whole packing list is summarized to no. of total boxes which are going in applicable shipping schedule ! When consignment scope is small, all parts can be sent in one shipping order ! If scope of the shipping consignment is huge, we have a system of partial shipping or phase wise shipping where material which is urgent at site activities is first manufactured and shipped and then next list is sent ! So, in phase wise shipping schedule, you have to clearly provide necessary details of all shipping essentials, like name of the customer, product being dispatched , project details , project dispatch address , scope of the consignment , its seal of inspection before packing clearance , documents involving permissions to send material outside territory from export import formalities, taxes applicable and taxes paid receipts , vehicle details and mandatory licenses for shipping of goods, inputs for unloading activities in port area and handing over of consignment to shipping agencies as per terms of contracts , when the material reaches site port , the receivers acknowledgement and payment details , the transportation from port to applicable site address , receipt of site and acceptance of goods received note along with processing of invoice for financial clearance from customer end , payment to customer either through cash , electronic clearance or bank guarantee as agreed in the terms of contract !

An ideal shipping process involves supplying material correctly and fully and receiving the material correctly and fully ! Any damage happened during the transportation is the responsibility of the transporter and necessary insurances need to be taken to cover the risks during shipping !

As far as corporate governance in shipping and commercial activities is concerned , when a product is ready for supply , the supplier has a comfortable dialogue with its purchaser and they both mutually and totally agree on supply of product ! If any party has any query , suggestion or question about product details , same need to be resolved before product being dispatched ! If you supply the product with your certificate and if errors are observed during receipt , then resolution is a costly affair and it affect your brand image ! Hence , if customer wants to see the product before it get dispatched , he has to make arrangement for his inspection at manufacturer's facility else manufacturer's test certificate is considered as silent clearance for purchaser and if any issue is there , it will be resolved with mutual co-operation !

13.3 Intelligent Commercial Prudence :

Image Courtesy: Frank Mckenna , Unsplash.com

When you are doing any kind of business , the basic requirement is its legal existence ! As far as customer- supplier –dealer relationship is concerned , for long term and lasting relations which enhance mutual co-operation and financial benefit , everyone has to set good terms of commercial agreement with each other before entering into business relation !

Business relations starts with a need and they get its true meaning when the need is fulfilled with total satisfaction ! Hence commercial terms are legal bindings on both parties or parties involved in contracts and hence from order initiation to complaint resolution , every action is done within the framework designed in commercial terms ! So , when you are entering into an offer or business relation , you have to understand each and every clause of the commercial agreement and you have to raise your doubts and query ! If you don't have any doubt or query and if you want to start the business relation , then you have to sign the agreement indicating the terms of contracts are acceptable and all clauses and conditions mentioned in the contract are legally binding on each party equally and independently as per the scope of service defined and agreed !

So commercial terms has various factors which can be final price of the product and its payment terms , warranty or guarantee of the product quality and its agreed timeline within which the repair or replacement are manufacturers responsibility , force-majeure clause where delay or supply of work because of circumstances beyond manufacturers control are noted and manufacturers will not be held responsible for consequences of force majeure , agreement for final quality and acceptance of test report , objections and no objections clause and its applicability , judicial approachability and area of jurisdiction as applicable to resolve any complaint about agreement , the clause of disagreement within both parties and charges of reimbursement on account of voluntary disagreement , penalty and LD clauses which makes sure the items or products are supplied on time and delays beyond agreed timeline are avoided , scope of responsibility of supplying products as per EXIM terms , it covers scope of shipment , its charges and its accountability !

Intelligent manufacturers try to specify their responsibility very very clearly ! They commit what they are supposed to commit and they do not own any additional responsibility which is applicable at customers end !

A genuine customer also knows their scope of purchasing a product and hence they will also not enforce any additional requirement at supplier end!

Before purchasing product , all commercial terms are well discussed with each other and then only after techno commercial agreement , the orders are booked and fulfilled within applicable delivery period which can be mentioned in number of hours , number of days , number of months , number of years or open ended delivery period when product is completely ready from manufacturers end !

So , when Good Corporate Governance is in place , there is less finish good in warehouse waiting for payment clearance from customer and lead time of order booking to total payment is consistently maintained after shipping of the product ! ✱✱✱

CHAPTER 14 : SITE WORK AND SITE VIGILANCE

" The main duty of site professionals is to maintain the quality of site scope and establish strong customer centric brand image! "

Image Courtesy: Etienne Giradet , Unsplash.com

14.1 Introduction:

Hello Friends,

In this chapter, we are going to see some of the important aspects of site work of supplied products and how it is performed to ensure the effective brand image of corporate governance! When site work is there, you need to follow same approach which you follow in shop work! System and discipline remains same in a good Corporate Governance!

14.2 Basic Corporate Governance in Site work:

Corporate Governance has a very very great role to play in administrating site environments! Let's see how the site work is managed and site vigilance is carried out point wise!

1) Basically site is referred as any workplace which is not your home workplace, its different work center or work unit where your supplied product will provide its intended service! In general, it's known as customer's premises!

2) Sites are external interfaces between customer and supplier! Here supplier reaches customers place to install products supplied by him either through a directly engaged and appointed service team or it can be through any third party servicing and installation team or franchise which is competent of handling the installations of products! So, whatever instructions for installing different products are there, they need to be applicable and actionable to available site environment!

Here trick of the site work is that, you can manufacture thousand standard parts having same dimensions and same features but site environment where you are installing it may have different environmental parameters in which your product is going to serve for long time!

Hence while designing your product , you have to take care that in applicable environmental conditions like humidity , melting point , boiling point , maximum allowable pressure and thickness limits, minimum allowable design temperature , density of material and flow rates of inside working material , properties of working material and its effect on your product , all these factors need to be considered well in advance by carrying out target market to which the products are designed to take care that your product will fulfill the required need of the environment !

So, as far as role of corporate governance is considered in site work and site vigilance, ensuring safety at site work and timely completion of installation activity within given time frame and site budget is important stand to support the huge or small work carried on regular basis!

3) Site budget is different than your in-house manufacturing budget! All the manufacturing activities are more or less similar but their applicable environment is different! Generally , site assembly work consist of uniform joining of overall solution system in which different parts are fitted as per engineering logic ! If you have created all parts correctly but if during site assembly, you unknowingly made any mistake, the effect on site performance can be easily felt!

Secondly, site work is carried out at different locations! The availability of trained and qualified manpower, required consumables and assembly fixtures, all you have to manage as per nature of your installation contract! In such cases, if you are hiring professional services, they are quite expensive and these expenses you need to consider before accepting purchase enquiry or you can quote these charges as additional charges when you are providing estimates of your service!

Corporate Governance has clear site policy across the organization! Here every functional and strategic manager is equipped with powers of approving bills and expenses that occur on account of customer installation services! When the product is new, these expenses are studied properly during its implementation stage, when the installation is completed, the whole budget of installation is calculated and accordingly for next jobs of similar type fine tuning is done with activities which are essential! Budget is reworked based on minimizing non-essential activities if carried out during first installation!

4) The main duty of site professionals is to maintain the quality of site scope and establish strong customer centric brand image! Being at customer premises, you are representing your organization and hence all professional code of conduct need to be followed through facilitator or mediator available with you from customers end! As you are working in customers safety environment , you have to take dual care that you follow all safety norms of customers working environment as well as you carry out your designated work safely so that it will not affect their in process activities ! If required, you need to take prior site permissions for temporarily closing the working place from human and machine intervention when site team is carrying out installation related activities which can be potentially risky! Here site safety officer from customer premises guides supplier site manager about basic essentials and allot necessary permissions of certain hours or certain time frame within which you have to complete your planned work so that their work also not get affected !

This type of mutual understanding you need to set by following good code of site conduct!

5) Every relation is special and business relation has great impact on professional development! Once you understand the customer's working environment and your general arrangement drawing, you get the idea of available place and part locations! Then you fit the required part at required place and join them in such a way that complete pre- performance check can be done! In pre-performance check, you measure the dimensions of complete assembly and their elevations as mentioned in electrical drawing or general assembly drawing! Electrical drawings guide you about flow of current through systems and hence you can easily locate position of switches and control panels! Once pre-performance check is done, you take a performance trail and observe how your product is functioning and how it is giving standard outcome expected from it!

6) In site vigilance, the role of corporate governance starts with developing habit of

safety culture and installing sense of social security while carrying out any site work! Site people come from different work rolls! They can be fixed resources or temporary resources, they can be on contract resources or can be apprentice in action, you have to understand the risk involved in site work and accordingly you have to depute trained and qualified manpower! Effect of any manhandling or unsafe condition at site initiates enquiry and audit trail which affect final commitment of handing over of site! Hence, first and foremost important thing to consider is getting work done safely!

7) Although site work is remote work, with the help of communication technology now all the site communication can be done on line to authorized person by following site safety protocols! Because of daily reporting, site vigilance become easier & it maintains safe brand image of the supplier! ✳✳✳

CHAPTER 15 : HUMAN RESOURCE DEVELOPMENT

" Hiring leadership role is always a notable corporate governance challenge! "

Image Courtesy: Van tay media , Unsplash.com

15.1 Introduction:

Hello Friends,

In this chapter, we are going to see fundamental aspects of human capital in any organization and the role of corporate governance in running the show with ultimate talent hired and performing in the system!

15.2 Need of Talent for Industry:

Image Courtesy: Sebastian Herrmann ,Unsplash.com

Every industry performs a creative activity that meets people need! When people create something either through individual contribution or team performance, the total effect of work is useful for others! Useful products and services makes work simple for users and hence are qualified for getting their value in the form of its purchase price ! Cohesive teams working with each other for the benefits of customers on supply of products earns descent money known as total turnover! When taxes and other liabilities of the business are paid out and all expenses are paid to individual parties, whatever remains is the profit after tax, depreciation, interest, and amortization! It is known as EBITDA!

So, when you have a well-qualified and talented team with you, the team performs well and meets their targets consistently! There are fewer chances of errors and even if they are made, team resolves them very very quickly! Hence the overall performance in creating and developing products is fantastic and hence amount of turnover is also huge! The profits earned are attractive and continuous contribution of profit ads up to reserves and surplus tally of the firm! That's why talented people are required in every industry to make mutual development and to have right kind of customer service!

15.3 Corporate Governance for management hiring:

Hiring leadership role is always a notable corporate governance challenge! You have to choose a person who is capable of handling your business on his own and with the help of systems equipped to serve well! They have to draft vision of the organization for long term and they have to complete the aimed target in stipulated time or earlier! While doing same, they have to maintain the work-life balance of team by nurturing the culture of the organization! Every leader has a task of inspiring and motivating his or her team to perform well and remain effective! Such big roles are hired through various hiring processes! Business networking is one of the widely used ways to go for leadership roles! Leaders need to have influence and hence leaders are hired through influential network of successful people!

Before hiring a leader , he need to have proven track record of best in the field , excellent people & communication skill and untiring zeal to challenge the status quo!

15.4 Corporate Governance for Senior Management to junior management roles:

In any organization, after the board of the director forming, the next big task is hiring senior, middle and junior managers to take care of the business functions! The board of the director is the body of eminent professionals in the business! There may be top notch consultants, experienced professionals, influential brands and retired officials! They usually take care of the investors and business interest! They know the market well and they also know the investment needs to foster the business in any environment in which they are working!

Senior management is the functional leaders and they guide their team to meet daily targets! These leaders have 25-30 years of experience in the field and they know the organization from long time! They are supporter of organization in all challenging situations and they have taken huge efforts through individual and team contribution to make sure that challenges are surpassed and growth of the unit is achieved!

Middle level managers are bridge between senior and junior level managers! Their role is to make missions possible! They always thrive to give specific directions to junior managers and they present review report to senior managers! The role of middle level managers is very very crucial in the organization! When there is need of the organization, they are always ready to accept the big responsibilities and at times, they can also develop junior level resources by sharing their experience and making work easy for junior level managers!

Junior level managers are people who are having experience of 5-10 years in the organization! They are regular in their approach and they know the system thoroughly! They are always on learning edge and middle level managers mentor them on challenging assignments! They may report to middle level managers or may report to senior level managers! They learn from everyone in the organization and they spend most of the time with executives in the filed who are driving force of any organization!

15.5 Corporate Governance for Senior Executives, Junior Executives and Trainees:

In any organization, this level of human capital is considered as future strength of the organization! They have experience of working up to 0- 5 or 7 years! They are field people and they are directly in contact with on field workers, operators, technicians, supporting aids and office staff! Their work nature is regular and they have to do what they are trained to do! Basically, their responsibilities are mixed! They are supposed to fulfill the prime responsibility as agreed in their role profile while they also have to develop their caliber to go for higher roles!

This age is extremely young age of the candidate and whatever you achieve in this age become your corporate identity after few years! In this age, you need to develop various skills as required to perform your job well! You also have to acquire various training and development certificates with which you can walk your career journey with immense pride and feeling of satisfaction! This talent is hired by middle level managers with approval of senior level managers which in turn sanctioned by business leader!

15.6 Corporate Governance for Skilled and semi-skilled workers and operators:

For any industrial set up, the actual manpower who is engaged to carry out daily work on the basis of daily wages is very very crucial and important! There are various business trades and training programmers through which these people are hired! They perform only specific task in which they are skilled and qualified! They can learn other task also but their main responsibility is to deliver the hired skill! They can be welder, fitters, plumbers, electricians, carpenters, foundry workers, machinist, meters, CNC operators, machine operators, crane operators!

Company- union of worker relation is an important business relation which is maintained by following terms and conditions of work contract and applicable labor laws and factory establishment act! Necessary facilities and safe working conditions are provided by the manufactures for this workforce so that required man-hours are generated and throughput is visible! They have fix working hours and in case of overtimes, they have to pay extra wages! Continuous skill development programs can be run to handle challenging jobs!

15.7 Corporate Governance for Non-technical support staff, clerical roles, administrative and security roles:

This is another important talent wing in any organization! They are non-technical people with basic qualification up to degrees such as BA, B.com, and BSc! Their roles are mainly documentation oriented and they support junior managers, executives and senior executives where they are appointed! Support staff is required! When you are singing a group song the strength of chorus adds to brilliance of the song, in same way, the support staff makes work simple! They can be hired by middle level managers and their direct reporting is given to junior managers!

Security of the firm is an important aspect of business and in current set up we need multi-level security system! We need to protect our physical assets, intellectual assets as well as our human capital from all types of risks and causalities! Hence we can hire chief security officer with his team! We can hire chief information officer along with his team! Maintaining secure environment is a team goal and everyone in the organization is responsible equally to keep the workspace safe and secure!

15.8 Corporate Governance for undefined roles, external service agencies and ad-hoc mediators:

When business experience several uncertainties, some people are called back having ample experience to deal with challenges! They know the difficulty and they have good hold on its solution! Company takes care to hire such professional services which are time bound and specific yet very very high profile opportunities! Every human is capital as far as corporate governance is concerned! ⊛

CHAPTER 16 : WORKFORCE MANAGEMENT

" Corporate roles are result oriented and business commitment has paramount importance! "

Image Courtesy : Alex Kotliarskyi , Unsplash.com

16.1 Introduction:

Hello Friends,

In this chapter, we are going to see, how workforce is managed with the help of principles of corporate governance! When working in an organizational network, there are certain roles and responsibilities with which individual and group contribution is assessed and awarded! Workforce management is important identity of corporate governance and professional managers are trained on regular basis to deal with live circumstances! Let's see, how workforce is managed!

16.2 Recruitments:

The first stage of workforce management through corporate governance is recruitment of people for specific roles and responsibilities! While delivering technical products, you have to follow a traditional sequence of input-processing – output generation! Secondly for creating something, you need designers who are exactly aware about requirements of useful and safe design!

So, basically, recruitments happen in creative and executive level! Some recruitment also happens for supporting roles! Depending upon nature of responsibility and competence, people are screened and interviewed to know their proven talent! Once interviewers are satisfied, they offer the responsibility in the form of a job offer having certain emoluments and perks package for associating with them!

The offer of recruitment has contractual terms which candidate has to read and accept if he wants to accept the offer! If they have some concerns, they can discuss and get role clarification before finalizing the offer!

Accepted offer has a joining date as per mutual agreement which can range from immediate joining to joining within a month or two-three month! Depending upon the availability of talent, urgency of the position and previous workload of candidate, these terms are decided! In case of urgent recruitment, priority is given with due respect of everyone's time! The better and available candidate is given necessary time for joining without hurry! Because, a month or two moths delay never hamper work scenario to great extent!

16.3 Replacements:

In workforce management, replacement is often considered as last option when a performer fails to execute his or her responsibilities even after regular feedback!

Corporate roles are result oriented and business commitment has paramount importance! Its business world and people have to respect each other's time! If given results are not achieved, you can analyse the causes and decide corrective action plan to remove those reasons! However, if still new problems are arising in the system, then the leader and his team is monitored closely for their performance! If anything unprofessional is observed, then the responsible and accountable team member or team leader is replaced by equally talented candidate and he or she has given opportunity to serve for the organization! Performance is key in the organization and people are always inspired to work hard to accomplish goals!

16.4 Terminations & Prohibitions:

One of the challenging task of managing workforce is enforcing a valid termination and prohibition! Sometimes because of unexpected incidences from human capital, organization terminates the services of human capital! The terminations can be individual or related to certain actionable group! Before any termination, due process of law as per internal system policy is followed and candidate may be informed or may be indirectly informed about the termination! To avoid future association, prohibitions are also suggested in a combined human capital platform!

Unlawful terminations experience penal charges when affected candidates approach suitable court and prove how his or her or their terminations are unlawful and because of which their name and other credentials are at stake! On hearing of both sides, honorary court gives their verdict and accordingly same is followed by both parties! It is therefore always advised that when you are hired for a role, always report your seniors about any unprofessional incidences happening at workplace!

16.5 Role changes and transfers:

Another important factor related to workforce management is allowing transfers and role changes to certain people! Working people are constantly monitored for their role and performance and they are supposed to report their work to their supervising managers! In case, you are performing well as per requirement of your role, you keep working in the same role for years until either manager or you don't ask for role change as per various business circumstances!

Every department and every role has a particular growth trajectory! It means , you can join as trainee , become executive , become senior executive , become assistant manager , become deputy manager , become manager , become senior manager , become divisional manager , become executive vice president , become president , become board of the director , become consultant ! The roles keep growing as you keep learning the organization's responsibility matrix! Depending on your role and your talent, you will be compensated or not compensated in the organization!

16.6 Promotions & Demotions:

Constantly performing people in the organization are appraised for their performance monthly, half yearly or annually and their performance feedback is given by their supervising managers! Based on their performance and applicable promotion policy, they are encouraged to offer bigger responsibilities with upgrade of compensation package! For some positions, promotions are indicators of unlimited growth potential while some promotions are extremely challenging job scenarios! Management most of the times make it clear that person getting promotion has required energy and competence to perform the assigned responsibility!

Demotions are negative growth indicators and in many respected organizations, demotions are discouraged! Instead of giving demotion, sensitive managers speak with candidate and find out special training need and then observe the improved performance! Industrial workforce is talented and if any skill gap is there, same can be filled by taking help of specialized training programs!

16.7 Retirements, Voluntary Retirements, Layoffs:

Business is legitimate process and while doing business certain social responsibilities have to be followed by both parties in service agreement! Basically job is a form of service for which you get paid by the company! There is term of service for fixed roles and generally superannuation age is decided in the service agreement! On attaining superannuation, you are discharged from your duties and responsibilities and accordingly you have given a retirement benefit package as a respect for your contribution in building the organization to great height in the timeframe you served!

There are certain number of people who get retire annually and with every passing year this number can grow or reduce! Based on company's future business forecast, management can recruit new people at vacant place, can promote existing people at vacant place or simply can run show with available workforce till the workload is under control of workforce! It's corporate governance decision and it is taken with due study of human capital requirement and current status! Human capital is considered as asset for the organization and hence long term recruitment is always the basic need before hiring new candidate! Recruitments takes their own time and its lengthy process, hence precautions are taken in hiring great talent for the organization after one's retirement! Because, you have to maintain the same leadership qualities and performance standards to keep the organization in active mode always! Predecessor and successor planning is altogether different corporate governance exercise which always happens with deep thought process before someone retires , because before retirement , you have to be ready with options of new candidate which can be interviewed and can be promoted to bigger responsibility! Generally, within a team, when the supervising manager retires, their charge is given to equivalent supervising manager working in other function and who has desired experience of particular department or the junior person working in the department and having sufficient experience to perform the role is promoted! In case, in-house talent is not available, organization can hire person from external recruiting facility services who can join the team and can adjust to organizational culture as per the offer received!

When the business experience some unhealthy conditions , then after respecting the business forecast and order status , with strong thoughtful mind they have to announce voluntary retirement schemes where a suitable compensation package can be given if employees leave their services voluntarily ! Generally, people with less service years available opt for voluntary retirement and people who are young and energetic accept the workload whatever it is till they can find alternate employment offer in other facilities! Ultimately its mutual contract and both parties can separate by following lawful process of separation with applicable compensation!

Layoffs are mass termination of services which can have notice period of one day or two-three month's as organization find it suitable after noting business scenarios! In challenging business scenarios where new orders are at halt and economic market is experiencing recession, organizations find it difficult to pay the salaries to employee without considerable output which can run the business! Hence layoffs are announced and huge number of human capital is communicated about discontinuation of their services form so and so date and time and accordingly they will be given applicable compensation as per employment contract! In some cases, three months' salary and other accumulated benefits are given! In unlawful layoffs, employee files case against the organization and keep waiting for justice till the verdict is given! Layoff is quite known action taken by organizations when business expects unhealthy conditions! Laid down workforce may find out other jobs or may start their own business or any external service facility with which they can take care of their personal responsibilities !

Every resource working in the business environment tries to fulfill his duties normally and as per agreed requirement! If any challenge is arrived, with the help of team efforts, same is resolved! Business is about interpersonal material need and both parties have to be fair and fine when they are committed!

16.8 Ex-Employees Welfare Management:

Organizations with deep social connect and commitment takes extreme step of taking care of their ex-employees when they are retired from service! On retirement, sufficient compensatory benefits are invested in various group saving schemes and pension funds so that they can receive respectable money per month even if they are not working for the organization! In some progressive organizations, employee's forms their welfare trust and makes deal with insurance agencies where their medical expenses post retirement can be taken care off with payment of equivalent premium when they are actually serving for the organization!

Few organizations, in their recruitment policy, give preference to close relatives of ex-employees who have distinguished service record in the organization! Many ex-employees can start their own small entrepreneurial activities and can provide their services to company for which they served! This role transition from employee to supplier is quite healthy and it gives ample opportunities of growing together with the organization for which you have served for number of years!

16.9 Supplier Development through internal resources:

When the limits of corporate governance occupy external territories, you need your people to get work done your way! It's as simple as that! There are few people who are very very ambitious and they keep finding new opportunities, they look for their career advancement by following untraditional paths! Such past employees are encouraged by the organization by developing their professional bonds in the form of faithful suppliers!

As a registered vendor with the firm, you already know the internal systems and major corporate policies! You are aware about various decision makers and you can approach internal business authorities with or without a formal appointment! Hence becoming registered vendor and supplying sub-contracting part is another form of work force management!

As business expands, you need more people and you focus on core work! The work which is supportive and less risky is sub contracted to qualified manufacturers and you keep proper control on quality aspects through implementing dedicated quality culture at their place! This way of doing business with your own suppliers is mutually beneficial and in the end you get known workforce which is serving from external territories!

16.10 Overseas Business Mediators and delegates:

When you expand your business in overseas market, you combine your workforce with inclusion of local talent! Local talent is in daily contact with local administration and hence managing business become easy! Business mediators and delegates make the regulatory framework easy for the organization which is expanding! This is the way workforce is managed in Corporate Governance! ⊛⊛⊛

CHAPTER 17: LABOUR LAWS & CORPORATE LAWS

" Justice is everyone's right and injustice in business relation affect its reputation and brand influence! "

Image Courtesy: Rahul Kashyap, Unsplash.com

17.1 Introduction:

Hello Friends,

In this chapter, we are going to see basic information about labor laws and corporate laws! Business being a legitimate activity, every stakeholder, owner, workmen and operators as well as any third party service provider comes under the umbrella of laws! Justice is everyone's right and injustice in business relation affect its reputation and brand influence! Hence , every businessman ,while incorporating their Corporate Governance always try to form a separate legal cell who can assist them in times of conflicts and unprofessional behaviors of person or group of person , occasionally or frequently in a way it affects regular business momentum ! Some logical stands are always encouraged by the authentic businessman's where demands are justified , however using rules and regulations for their mis interpretation and unlawful application always deteriorate business and personal relation which result into non-cooperation , separation and jobless ness which is exactly contradictory to core business value of mutual development and mutual support ! Let's understand some of the labor laws first so that corporate laws can be discussed later.

17.2 Labor Laws:

1) Minimum Wages Act 1948

This act is about making provision of minimum wages to be paid to workmen as set by government when he delivers his work! This act also limits working week up to 40 hours (9 hours a day with 30 minute break in between)

(*Ref: Indian Labor Law, Wikipedia*)

2) The Payment of Wages Act 1936

This act is about making payment on last day of the month either through bank transfer or through postal services.

(*Ref: Indian Labor Law, Wikipedia*)

3) Factories Act 1948 & Shops and Establishment Act 1960

Mandates 15 fully paid vacation leaves and 7 sick leaves annually to each employee!

(Ref: Indian Labor Law, Wikipedia)

4) Maternity Benefit (Amendment) Act 2017

This act gives right to every female employee of every company to take 6 month's fully paid maternity leave! In case of medical termination of pregnancy or miscarriage, they are allowed to take 6 weeks full paid leave!

(Ref: Indian Labor Law, Wikipedia)

5) Employee Provident Fund and Miscellaneous Provisions Act 1952

This works as generating pension fund after retirement! Here employee and employer both contribute 10-12% basic salary per month in the account opened with Employee provident fund organization and same is paid after retirement. Deposited money can be withdrawn for several life needs as communicated in provisions of provident funds!

(*Ref: Indian Labor Law, Wikipedia*)

6) The Industrial relation code 2020, the code on social security 2020, the occupational safety, health and working conditions code 2020, Code on wages 2019

These codes constitute 44 existing labor laws and take care of social and occupational security of the labor's employed in various industries!

(*Ref: Indian Labor Law, Wikipedia*)

7) Employee state insurance act 1948

According to this act, employees are entitled to take 90 days of paid leaves for medical emergency or medical reasons!

(*Ref: Indian Labor Law, Wikipedia*)

8) The Industrial Employment Act 1946

This law includes employment terms such as working hours, leaves, productivity goals, dismissal procedure approved by government! It also contains non-disclosure agreement clause, non-compete clause and confidentiality clause!

(*Ref: Indian Labor Law, Wikipedia*)

9) Industrial Dispute Act 1947

This old act is updated in 1948 act and additional 45 national laws expands and 200 state laws controls the employee-employer Interaction which includes points of 6 attendance logs, 10 accounts for overtime and 5 files of annual returns! Workplace need to be clean and there is provision in law regarding height of urinals in workers washroom to how many time the workplace need to be clean! Observations are subjected to inspector's remark and necessary law enforcement!

(*Ref: Indian Labor Law, Wikipedia*)

10) The contract labor act 1970

This act is made for contract labor to provide them lawful rights of contract employment!

(*Ref: Indian Labor Law, Wikipedia*)

11) The Minimum Wages Act 1948

This law sets wages for different economic sectors which are running in states!

(*Ref: Indian Labor Law, Wikipedia*)

12) Payment of Gratuity Act 1972

For organizations employing more than 10 employees, payment of 15 days salary per year of service served is mandatory to be paid if employee retires or resigns! The maximum gratuity amount applicable is 20, 00,000!

(*Ref: Indian Labor Law, Wikipedia*)

13) The payment of Bonus Act 1965

For organizations employing more than 20 employees, payment of bonus on annual performance and profit collection is mandatory. 8.33 % of salary needs to be paid as bonus for that year!

(Ref: Indian Labor Law, Wikipedia)

14) Weekly holiday Act 1942

This act is made for providing grant for weekly holidays to person employed in the organization!

(Ref: Indian Labor Law, Wikipedia)

15) Beedi & Cigar workers Act, 1966

This act is made for welfare of workers serving this field and it also provides clauses for safe working conditions!

(Ref: Indian Labor Law, Wikipedia)

16) Workmen's compensation act 1923

The compensation to be paid to workers in case they get injure during working. The rates are low!

(Ref: Indian Labor Law, Wikipedia)

17) Occupational safety, health and working conditions code 2020

This code is for amending and consolidating laws related to occupational safety, health and working conditions for person employed in the organization.

(Ref: Indian Labor Law, Wikipedia)

18) The sexual harassment of women at workplace Act 2013

This act is made for protecting women in the workplace and also providing a mechanism by which they may report incidences of sexual harassment in the workplace!

(Ref: Indian Labor Law, Wikipedia)

19) Unorganized workers social security act 2008

This act is made for unorganized workers such as home workers, self-employed workers, daily wage workers for their welfare and social security!

(*Ref: Indian Labor Law, Wikipedia*)

20) Trade Unions Act 1926

This act amended in 2001 contains rules of governance and rights of trade unions!

(*Ref: Indian Labor Law, Wikipedia*)

21) Industrial relations code 2020

This code amended and consolidated central labor laws regarding trade unions, conditions of employment in establishments and settlement of industrial dispute!

(*Ref: Indian Labor Law, Wikipedia*)

22) Constitutional articles for equality

Article 14- Everyone is equal before law

Article 15 – State should not discriminate citizens

Article 16- Equality for opportunity in the employment

Article 23 – Forced labor and trafficking prohibited

Article 24 – Child labor below age 14 is not allowed in factory, mine or any hazardous establishments!

Article 39d – Equal pay for equal work irrespective of gender discrimination.

Transgender persons Act 2019 – Bans discrimination on gender identity in the employment.

Scheduled caste and scheduled tribe Act (Prevention of atrocities) 1989

Bans discrimination on the basis of caste in employment and trade!

Bonded labor Act 1976

This act abolishes bonded labor who can be debt bonded!

Fair Dismissal clause in Industrial dispute act 1947:

Employer needs government permission & necessary approval before firing workmen who is employed for more than a year in the organization!

Clause for redundancy payment:

An employee before retrenchment has to give 15 days' average pay for each complete year of continuous service! An employee served for more than 4 years with all notices and due process must be paid minimum of the employees wage equivalent to 60 days before retrenchment!

(*Ref: Indian Labor Law, Wikipedia*)

23) Industries Act 1951

Manufacturing industries in act's first schedule will be in control of common central regulations along with state laws .This act reserved over 600 products that can be manufactured in small scale enterprise. This limits who can enter in the business! Also, there is limit on number of people employed in these businesses!

(*Ref: Indian Labor Law, Wikipedia*)

24) State laws:

Every Indian state based on central act forms state laws and approved it in state legislation! From state to state, these laws can be different, so united, there are number of state laws according to each state! These state laws commonly classified as laws related to wages, social security, occupational health and safety and industrial relations!

State laws for explanation, Case 1 – Industrial dispute act amendment in 2004 in Gujarat for flexibility of labor market in the SEZ of Gujarat - With this amendment, companies within SEZ can lay off redundant workers without government approval and by issuing notice and severance pay!

State laws for explanation, Case 2 – Revision in labor laws is made in such a way in west Bengal that it will be virtually impossible for loss making companies to shut down completely!

So, different state can form their state laws in accordance with central act!

In the first part of this chapter, we have seen labor laws existing in India for the overall welfare, safe working conditions and protection of civil rights of workmen serving in organized and unorganized sectors! Before law everyone is equal and Indian laws take care of maintaining freedom, brotherhood and equality principles in the formation and execution of laws by following due process of law whenever such instances occurs!

These laws cover industrial relations and internal environment inside any organization! But what about external environment! A businessman has to face this external environment also in same way as he deals with internal environment! Because we all are part of a universal system called as market and it's our working duty to serve these markets by catering to its needs! While doing our duties, we have to ensure, we remain faithful to each other and we make products which are helpful to society without causing hazard to internal or external environment! In this regard, let's see laws which take care of business-customer relation in the form of corporate laws!

(*Ref: Indian Labor Law, Wikipedia*)

Corporate Laws:

1) The Companies Act 1956

This act explains the necessary basics related to formation of companies and its governing board along with description of rights and duties of functional roles. The act speaks in details about major corporate terms like board of directors, managing director, share capital , holdings, financial institutions, public limited company, private company, powers of authorities, manager and managers role , dividend , vote of trust , annual general meeting , debt and equity capital!

　　With the help of this act, one can easily note the exact legal identity of the firm and its role in interaction with market! Company creates products and sells in the market! Thus through years spend in the business company achieves profit and create capital for business. This capital further can be increased by allowing public to buy the shares of the company with monetary investment. Based on company performance, dividends are offered to investors! All the details of limited liability of stakeholders are available in the act!

There are types of companies which can be sole proprietorship, private company, limited liability Company, public limited company! The nature of business and distribution of decision making powers especially related to operational and financial domain are defined in each form of company to have understanding of span and control of business!

Financial powers and its distribution is key concern in corporate governance! Through this act, concern authorities and their approval powers are clearly specified!

In the event of major corporate decisions, the board of directors has concentration of powers and distribution of powers! Act specifies the powers associated with board of directors!

Basically , this act is about adhering to all legal requirements pertaining to business identity in the market because company is artificial person in the legal world which is run by natural people through roles and responsibility in order to have financial turnover for sales of goods & services !

(*Ref : Indian corporate law service, Wikipedia*)

2) Companies Act 2013

This act has one specialty! Here one person can also form the company in the form of OPC! Apart from this provision, the act has following chapters!

Chapters on formation of incorporations.
Chapters of raising authorized share capital.

Chapters on management of administration.

Chapters on accounts of companies.

Chapters about company audits.

Chapters about appointment of directors, managing directors, their meetings and their qualification.

Chapters about judicial arrangement and industrial tribunals.

Chapters about government companies, producer companies, companies outside India. Chapters on inspection, inquiry, investigation.

Chapters on revival and rehabilitation of sick companies.

Chapters on winding up of companies with liquidation process.

Chapters on furnishing information and statistics.

(Ref : Indian corporate law service, Wikipedia)

3) Provision of Indian Corporate Law service

Indian corporate law services – ICLS is central civil services (Group A) under the ministry of corporate affairs, Government of India! This service is entrusted for implementation of corporate acts like – company's act 1956, company's act 2013 and limited liability partnership act 2008!

ICLS provides its services according to following roles

Junior time scale like Assistant registrar of companies

Senior time scale like deputy registrar of company

Junior administrative grade like joint director

Selection grade –nonfunctional like director to the government of India through central staffing services.

Senior administrative grade like regional director.

Higher administrative grade like director general of corporate affairs!

(Ref: Indian corporate law service, Wikipedia)

4) Limited liability partnership act 2008

This act contains details of partnership firms with their limited liability of financial matters in relation to nature of the business. Earlier, we have Indian partnership act 1932. LLP is body of corporate and legal entity separate from its partners, it has perpetual succession and any change in the partners does not affect its existence! This new act has following key points in its clauses.

Nature & incorporation of limited liability companies

Partners, their relation, extent and limitation on partner's liability.

Contributions and financial disclosures.

Assignment and transfer of partnership rights.

Investigation.

Conversion to limited liability partnership, foreign limited liability partnerships.

Compromise, arrangement or reconstruction of limited liability companies.

Winding up and dissolution, miscellaneous!

(*Ref : Indian corporate law service, Wikipedia*)

5) Indian Partnership Act 1932

This act is about business in partnership where partners has to work for common advantage , they have to be true to each other and all accounts and information of the business has to be given by each partner to each other , their legal heir or legal representative whenever such requirements get generated!

(Ref: mca.gov.in)

6) Consumer protection act 1986

This act is enacted for protection of consumer's interest and giving them an opportunity to present before the consumer protection court to file their concerns on products or services consumed. Consumers can also form consumer councils to make their voice strong and clear!

(Ref: legislative.gov.in)

7) Environment Protection Act 1986

This act covers all types of pollution like air, water, soil and noise. It provides safe standards for presence of various pollutants in the environment. It prohibits use of hazardous material unless permission is taken from central government.

All industries have to obey the guidelines given in the act and they have to ensure that necessary audits and compliances are maintained in their routine operations!

(*Ref: Indiacode.nic.in*)

8) The Foreign Trade (Development & Regulation) Act ,1992

This act is made for the development and regulation of foreign trade by importing into India and augmenting export from India , matters related to foreign trade and incidental happenings thereto !

(*Ref: Indiacode.nic.in*)

Earlier we have Import-Export (Control) Act 1947

The main chapter in the foreign trade (Development and Regulation) Act, 1992 are

Power of central government to make order and announce foreign trade policy.

Importer- exporter code number and license

Quantitative restrictions

Search, seizure, penalty and confiscation.

Controls on export of specified goods, services and technology.

Appeal and review, miscellaneous.

(*Ref: prsindia.org*)

9) Intellectual property act

Business is done on the basis of intellectual ability of an individual and hence intellectual property in various forms like copyrights, trademark, logo, design need to be protected as firm's exclusive property! This protection is provided by following intellectual property law mainly known as IP laws!

The Patents act 1970, Amendments – 1999, 2002, 2005

Protection of plant varieties and farmers right act 2001

The semiconductor Integrated circuits layout design act 2000

The design act 2000

Copyright act 1957 & amendment 1994, 1999

The Geographical Indications of Goods (Registration and protection) Act, 1999

The Trademarks act 1999

(*Ref: icsi.edu*)

10)   The Information Technology act 2000

With rising use of information technology in all forms of business for electronic transaction of goods and service related information, for protection of transactional information and sensitive confidential data, the IT act 2000 is enacted which host related IT laws! The matters of cyber security, cybercrimes and cyber frauds are covered in the act. The main purpose of act is to have legal recognition of electronic commerce and facilitate filing of electronic records! The laws covers four main rules related to contract, intellectual property, data protection and privacy! The act is amended in the year 2008!

(*Ref: eprocure.gov.in*)

11) The Income Tax Act 1961

This income tax act 1961 contains 298 sections and 14 schedules. It came into effect from 1 April 1962 with aim of identifying a taxpayer's taxable income, tax debt, appeals, files and legal troubles! According to this act, person having taxable income get their tax deducted at source and same is filed to Income Tax office in designated center. Tax payer has to file annual return to get their tax in return if he or she qualifies for return or the proofs of return filing to be keep handy for other commercial subjects such as matters related to loan approval from nationalized banks! Permanent account number is the income tax payer identity and before deducting tax, PAN no is essential! In the same way, companies have TAN number by which they deduct tax from their tax paying employees at source and provide TDS record to individual annually and through each month's salary slip. Delay in the payment of income tax or not filing return on time has adverse effect and related notices are given to concern tax payers or firms. (*Ref : incometaxindia.gov.in*)

12) Whistleblower act 2014

The act was approved by cabinet of India as a part of a drive to eliminate the corruption in the country's bureaucracy. The act covers wrong doing in the form of frauds, corruption or mismanagement! Act also provides punishment for false complaints.

There are two types of whistle blowing

Internal whistle blowing – Employee reports internal misconduct or incidences of corruption to designated competent authority.

External whistle blowing – Employee reports internal misconduct or corruption to external agencies like legal firms, media or the police.

Benefits of whistle blowing are follows

It provides confidential support service.

Everyone can access this support.

Misconduct gets reported.

Services can be expected as per standard requirement

(Ref: Whistle blower protection act_2011, Wikipedia)

13) GST Act 1999

A new tax system provides administrative framework for Goods and services tax (GST) law.

GST was primarily established under the 101st constitution amendment act 2016. The GST was launched at the midnight session of both houses by the president of the India and Government of the India on 1 July, 2017.

GST is further governed by CGST, SGST & IGST.

GST shall subsume various existing taxes across the country and introduce a single taxation system that will allow business to conduct business across the country by paying uniform taxes.

Before the introduction of GST, there were following tax laws which are necessary to know.

Central excise duty and duties of excise

Additional duties of excise and custom

Special additional duties of customs

Cess, state VAT, central sales tax.

(*Ref: Goods and services Tax (India),Wikipedia*)

14) Explosive substance Act 1908

This act provides power to central government to prohibit the manufacture, possession or importation of especially dangerous explosives. Various punishments are framed for type of unlawful action related to use of explosives. Companies when manufacturing good and catering to services need to ensure that interim or final products does not have any explosion like effect during their operations ! All due care need to be taken to protect the environment from risk hazards associated with explosive substances.

(*Ref: indiacode.nic.in*)

15) The Drugs and Cosmetics Act 1940

The drugs and cosmetics act 1940 is an act of parliament of India which regulates the import, manufacture and distribution of drugs in India. The primary objective of the act is to ensure that drugs and cosmetics sold in India are safe, effective and conform to state quality standards.

India has extensive network of pharmaceutical companies which counts to nearly 3000 in numbers along with more than 10,000 drugs, vaccine manufacturing facilities with availability of skilled workforce!

(*Ref: The drugs and cosmetics Act 1940, Wikipedia*)

16) Petroleum Act 1934 :

Petroleum act is an act to consolidate and amend the law relating to the import, transport, storage, production, refining and blending of petroleum! There are 5000 oil companies in India whereas the world host 1, 60,000 oil & gas companies! India is third largest consumer of petroleum products after US & China! India imports about 85 % of its petroleum products demand! In 2020-21, Indians refineries produced 221.37 Mt of oil which is 88. 8% of its refining capacity. IOCL refined 62.35 Mt of oil as a top oil producer in the nation!

(*Ref: petroleum.nic.in & Wikipedia*)

17) Indian Power Alcohol Act 1948 & Indian Power Alcohol Act (Repeal) 2000

This act is about production of power alcohol. No person shall manufacture power alcohol from any substance other than molasses or such other substance as may be specified by the central government.

(*Ref: indiacode.nic.in*)

18)   Indian Sugar cane act 1934

India becomes global leader of sugar producer as well as consumer surpassing Brazil! Indian sugar cane act 1934 regulates price of the sugar cane intended for use in sugar industries. In India, Uttar Pradesh ranks as top sugar producer followed by Maharashtra! The sugar production of India rose from 110 million tons in 1961 to 405 million tons in 2019!

There are around 732 sugar industries in India as on 31 July, 2017 out of which 327 are co-operative, 362 are private and 43 are public sector industries. Sugar industries are important part of agro based business which employs around 5 lakhs workers directly in sugar industries and sugar sector takes care of livelihood of around 50 million sugar cane farmers living in rural or urban regions ! Indian sugar mill association- ISMA estimates sugar production in 2022-23 year as 34.5 million tons!

Apart from this co-generation systems produce both electrical and thermal energy from same primary energy source. In a cogeneration plant very high efficiency level of 75-90 % can be reached to create heat and electrical energy. The sugar industry in India has a potential of 3500 MW to export to the grid. Extensive research is going on in the sugar industry to tap co-gen potential of Indian sugar industry along with production of ethanol! Out of 442 crore liter ethanol's contracted value in 2022 season, around 362 crore liters will come from sugar industry. Production of ethanol in sugar industry affects sugar production in respective seasons; hence ISMA declares seasonal sugar production capacity after accessing distribution of cane juice and B- molasses for production of ethanol.

(*Ref: dfpd.gov.in*)

19) Fertilizer Act 1994

Fertilizer act enacted for regulation and control of manufacture, processing, importation and sale of agricultural fertilizers and farm feed to provide minimum standards of effectiveness and purity of such fertilizers and feed. Act is also applicable for matters incidental or connected in relation to fertilizers foregoing!

(*Ref. : fert.nic.in*)

20) Insecticides act 1968

This act is enacted to regulate import, manufacture, sale, transport, distribution and use of insecticides with a view to prevent risk to human beings and animals and for matters connected therewith.

(*Ref: indiacode.nic.in*)

21) Construction Contract Act 2013

The provisions of the construction act 2013 provide subject to some exceptions, new legal rights and obligations on parties in the construction contract. The act imposes new minimum contractual provisions in relation to payments arising under a construction contract.

(Ref: mca.gov.in)

22) The real estate act 2016

With booming real estate industry inside the country and overall in the globe , the real estate act (Regulation & Development) 2016 aims to regulate and promote the real estate sector by regulating the transactions between buyers and promoters of residential as well as commercial projects.

(Ref: mohua.gov.in)

23) B2B e-commerce legislation

This legislation governs foreign investment and setting up of business in India by foreign entities and individuals is the prevailing Foreign Direct Investment Policy (FDI Policy) and the Foreign

Exchange Management Act 1999 with the accompanying rules.

(*Ref: mea.gov.in*)

24) The Textile Committee Act 1963

An act to provide for the establishment of a committee for ensuring the quality of textiles and textile machinery and for matters connected therewith.

(*Ref: indiacode.nic.in*)

25) The Indian Motor Vehicle Act 1988

The motor vehicle act is an act of parliament of India which regulates all aspects of road transport vehicles. The act provides in detail the legislative provisions regarding licensing of drivers/ conductors, registration of vehicles, control of motor vehicles through permits, special provisions relating to state transport undertakings, traffic regulation , insurance, liability, offenses and penalty .

(*Ref: motor vehicles act, Wikipedia*)

26) Iron and Steel companies amalgamation act 1952

An act to make special provision, in the interest of general public and the union, for the amalgamation of certain companies closely connected with each other in the manufacture and production of iron and steel, and for matters connected therewith or incidental thereto.

(Ref: thc.nic.in)

27) Essential commodities act 1955

An act to provide in the interest of general public , for the control of production, supply and distribution of , and trade of commerce in certain commodities .

Commodities covered include:

Fertilizers, Pulses, Edible oil, Cereals, Oilseeds, Petroleum and allied products, Seeds of fruits and vegetables.

In 2020 the act is modified as Essential Commodities (Amendment) Act 2020.

(*Ref: indiacode.nic.in*)

28) The Mines and Minerals (Development and Regulation) Amendment Bill 2021

This bill amends the mines and minerals (Development and Regulation) Act, 1957. The act regulates the mining sector in India. Regulation of labor and safety in mines is prime concern of this act.

(*Ref: ibm.gov.in*)

29) Indian Boiler Act , 1923

Indian Boiler Act, 1923 provides for the safety of life and property of persons from the danger of explosion of boilers. With Indian Boiler Regulation 1950, working pressure allowed for various parts of the boiler is specified. Provision of steam pipes and fittings is specified. Registration or Erection of boiler along with its inspection including inspection of pipe line is specified. Competent person may be allowed to inspect and certify the boilers during manufacture and use.

(*Ref : indiacode.nic.in*)

30) List of Environmental Laws

While carrying out business operations, regular contact with environmental elements become essential and while making profits from the business operation and by employment of manpower, one has to take care that the surrounded environment and climate remain unaffected because of various process waste in the form of solid, liquid or gaseous form. Various environment protection laws are formed in the nation. Let's know the name of these acts. On disobedience of these laws, business may encounter lawful provisions and actions made for protection of wellbeing in the larger interest of our environment.

The wildlife protection act 1972

The Water (Prevention and control of Pollution) Act 1974

The forest conservation act, 1980

The Air (Prevention and control of Pollution) Act, 1981

The Environment protection act, 1986

Public liability Insurance act, 1991

The biological diversity act, 2002

The national green tribunal act, 2010

(*Ref: iced.cag.gov.in*)

31) The Indian Green Building Council - IGBC

The IGBC is the leading green building movement in the country. Green building uses less water, optimizes energy efficiency, conserves natural resources, generates less waste and provides healthier spaces for occupants as compared to a conventional building.

This is not a law or an act, this council on application assesses a building based on 5 major categories totaling for 100 points.

Globally LEED – Leadership in Energy and Environment design is widely used for green building rating system.

(*Ref: igbc.in*)

32) Mental Healthcare Act 2017

As far as current lifestyle changes and job expectations are considered apart from many other life challenges like future security, health concerns, loans and payments, travel stress and traffic noise, many people are suffering from various mental stress symptoms. The mental health issues can start from talking less, possessing lack of confidence, forgetting the work, making mistakes, not doing work on time, too much expectations in comparison to ability to fulfill! People are undergoing chronic depression attacks and in the extreme event committing suicides. Considering the seriousness of matter and overall wellbeing of resource, mental healthcare act 2017 is passed.

According to this act , person with mental health issue can access related healthcare services , admission of person with mental illness has to follow certain guidelines according to this act   , this act decriminalizes suicide attempt made by such person   and prohibit electroconvulsive therapy , for minors ECT will not be performed   , responsibility of certain other agency is defined like police , own residence or home for homeless person where such person can expect rehabilitation, financial punishment is granted when the provisions of this act are not followed .

(*Ref: indiacode.nic.in*)

33) The Legal Metrology (Packaged Commodities) Rules 2011

It regulates prepackaged commodities in India and inter-alia mandate certain labeling requirements prior to sale of such commodities.

Whereas legal meteorology act 2009 establish and enforce standards of weight and measures, regulate trade and commerce in weights, measures and other goods which are sold or distributed by weight , measure or number and for matters connected therewith or incidental thereto .

(*Ref: consumeraffairs.gov.in*)

34) Indian Fisheries Act 1897

This act is made to provide protection, conservation and development of fisheries in the state and for matters connected therewith or incidental thereto.

Indian coastline is long and it measures around 7516 Km! Fish production date as of year 2022 shows 16248 tons of fish production. India hosts 3827 fishing villages and 1914 traditional fish landing centers! As of 2021-22 India ranks second largest fishing producer in the world. Around 280 lakh people win their livelihood through fisheries in India in Primary region; apart from this figure almost double population is available for subsequent value chain and distribution! Fisheries and aquaculture are showing rising growth prospectus in India!

(*Ref: pib.gov.in & Wikipedia*)

35) Mission for Integrated development of Horticulture (MIDH) and Maharashtra Horticulture Development Corporation Act ,1984

The Indian greenhouse horticulture market held a market value of USD 190.84 Million in 2021.

MIDH is centrally sponsored scheme for holistic growth of the horticulture sector covering fruits, vegetables, root & tuber crops, mushrooms, spices, flowers, aromatic plants, coconut, cashew, cocoa and Bamboo!

In Indian states except north east and Himalaya region, central contributes 60% scheme amount while state contributes 40 %, while in north east and Himalaya region central contributes 90% scheme amount.

Maharashtra Horticulture Development Corporation Act 1984 is made to make a special provision for securing the orderly establishment in horticulture production in the state of Maharashtra and for storage, transport, processing and marketing of horticulture produce and to assist generally in the organization thereof and for the purpose of establishing Maharashtra Horticulture Development corporation and for incidental and supplemental purposes connected with the matters aforesaid.

Horticulture account around 30% share of India's agricultural GDP. There are more than 174 horticulture companies and more than 955 agro companies in India!

(Ref: midh.gov.in & worldbank.org)

36) The Cigarettes and other tobacco products act 2003

The Cigarettes and other tobacco products (Prohibition of advertisement and regulation of trade and commerce, production, supply and distribution) Act 2003 or COTPA ,2003 is an act to prohibit advertisement of ,and to provide for the regulation of trade and commerce in , and production , supply and distribution of cigarettes and other tobacco products in India .

Indian cigarette market size reached USD 21.5 Billion in 2022 whereas India is second largest producer of tobacco products after china.

On global scale around 10% of cultivation area of tobacco production is in India!

There are around 14, 61,427 cancer patients in India! Consumption of tobacco and tobacco products like cigarettes is main reason of getting affected with deadly disease like cancer apart from consumption of liquor.

As per National Family Health Survey -5 carried out in 2019-20, male consumption of tobacco is observed ranging from 16.9% in Kerala to 72.9 % in Mizoram. Whereas women tobacco consumption is observed to be 1.7% in Himachal Pradesh to 61.6 % in Mizoram.

(Ref: Indiacode.nic.in & ibef.org)

37) The Indian Forest Act , 1927

This act is made to consolidate the law relating to forests, the transit of forest produce and the duty leviable on timber and other forest produce.

Forest produce is categorized into three types which are timber products, non-timber products and minor minerals!

States like Kerala, Punjab, Andhra Pradesh, West Bengal, Uttar Pradesh host important wood industries.

Major forest produce consist of timber, charcoal, wood-oil, resin, flowers and fruit, wild animals, skin , tusks, horns, bones, silk, honey, wax, surface soil, rocks and minerals !

India is leading exporter of Guar gum, shellac and sesame seeds! Apart from this, India is second largest exporter for medicinal plant in the world!

(*Ref: nbaindia.org*)

38) The Aircraft Act, 1937

This is an act made to make better provisions for the control of the manufacture, possession, use, operation, sale, import and export of aircraft.

India is worlds 9 th largest aviation market. It handles around 121 million domestic and 41 million international passengers. More than 85 international airlines operate to India and 5 Indian carriers connect over 40 countries.

Indian aerospace and defense composite market is forecasted to grow with 5% CAGR to 23 Billion USD. Karnataka is referred to as Aeronautic Hub of the India with its state capital Bengaluru having IAL's head quarter!

(*Ref: civilaviation.gov.in & ibef. Org*)

39) Manufacture , Storage and Import of Hazardous Chemical (Amendment) Rules, 1989

It regulates the manufacture, storage and import of hazardous chemicals in India. The transport of hazardous chemicals must meet the provisions of the motor vehicle act, 1988

Indian chemical sector employs nearly 2 million people and in the year 2021-2022, export of organic and inorganic chemicals increased by 38.67 % to reach USD 24,313.88 Million!

The production of chemical involves converting raw materials such as fossil fuels, water, minerals, and metals and so on into tens to thousand different products which are need of modern lifestyle!

(*Ref: thc.nic.in & ibef.org*)

40) The Arms Act , 1959

An act to consolidate and amend the law relating to arms and ammunition.

India has a domestic defense industry of which around 80% is government owned. The public sector includes DRDO and its 50 labs, 4 defense shipyards, 12 defense PSU's

The essential defense services act 2021 provide for the maintenance of essential defense services so as to secure security of the nation and life and property of public at large and for matters connected therewith or incidental thereto.

So, here one act supports other act! Under the essential defense services act Indian law assures protection of nation and with arms act

1959 , it consolidate and amend law relating to arms and ammunition in the interest of national security .

(*Ref: vifdatabase.com & Wikipedia*)

41) The Electricity Act ,2003

The electricity act 2003 is an act to consolidate the laws relating to transmission , distribution, trading and use of electricity and generally for taking measures conducive to development of electrical industry , promoting competition therein , protecting interest of consumers and supply of electricity to all areas, rationalization of electricity tariff, ensuring transparent policies regarding subsidies, promotion of efficient and environmentally benign policies, constitution of Central Electricity Authority, Regulatory commissions and establishment of Appellate Tribunal and for matters connected therewith or incidental thereto !

The electrical equipment market contains products like cables, switchgears, boilers, transformers and other products. Market also has generation, distribution and transmission category as per application of electrical products. The market is expected to grow by 9% CAGR by the year 2025 accounting to market size of USD 33.74 Billion!

India has 269 thermal power plants out of which 138 plants are in public sector while 131 plants are in private sector. India, as on year 2022, India has 22 nuclear reactors in operation at sites having an installed capacity of 6780 MW. At around 11 different locations, future nuclear power plants are planned!

(*Ref:cercind.gov.in & Wikipedia*)

42) The Atomic Energy Act , 1962

This is an act to provide for the development, control and use of atomic energy for the welfare of the people of India and for the peaceful purposes and for matters connected therewith.

India shows promising future in developing nuclear energy plants for generation of electrical energy. Currently as on 2021, India has 6.8 GW of installed nuclear energy capacity and as of December 2022, India is constructing capacity around 8.7 GW of nuclear energy plants. Over 80 GW plant capacities are under planned prospectus to meet energy needs of the future.

The risks associated with nuclear energy plant are related to high radiation emitting from radioactive sources and hence their careful handling during nuclear energy production. Uranium is major resource used in the production of nuclear energy and its mining requires extensive care during its complete presence on this planet!

Nuclear energy plants in India are controlled by Nuclear power Corporation of India (NPCIL). Also Bhartiya Nabhikiya Vidyut Nigam Limited (BHAVINI) authorized for production of electrical energy from nuclear energy in India . Both corporations are public undertakings of people of India !

(Ref:aerb.gov.in & pib.gov.in)

43) e- waste management rules in India ,2016

The Government of India (GOI) introduced the E-waste management rules in 2016. The rules apply to businesses that are generating electronic waste items . The most important legislation directly dealing with electronic waste is the Environment (Protection) Act ,1986. The major electronic wastes as per their category includes – Refrigerators, computers, telecommunication equipment's, consumer electronic devices and solar panel, TV's ,monitors, screens, LED bulbs, Vending Machines ! India's electronics production account to around 80 billion ! The global leader in the electronics industry is Germany ! Germany's FDI ranks seventh position in India's overall FDI tally . There are more than 1700 German companies operate in India in sectors associated with transportation, electrical equipment, metallurgical industries, services sectors like insurance, chemicals, construction activity , trading and automobile . IT act ,2000 is also there for the matters related with electronics and information technology !

(Ref:cpcb.nic.in & investindia.gov.in)

44) The Indian Energy Conservation Act, 2001

The energy conservation act 2001 was enacted to provide for efficient use of energy and its conservation and for matters connected therewith . This act provides for the establishment and incorporation of the Bureau of Energy Efficiency (BEE)

India's total installed electrical energy capacity is 4,11,649 as per CEA's (Central Electrical Authority's) data as of Jan-2023! In this sector ,there is center's contribution up to 24.2% , state contributes to 25.4 % and private sector contributes to 50.4 % .

Energy generation from fossil fuel accounts to 57.4 % , total non-fossil fuel accounts to 42.5 % .

Several initiatives are taken by ministry of power , government of India related to energy conservation . Some of the initiatives are –

1) Standards and labeling of equipment and appliances .

2) Energy conservation building code –ECBC

3) Demand side management scheme . Demands are further classified as agricultural demands, municipal demands . Initiatives like capacity building in DISCOMS- distribution companies - are taken to meet peak electricity demands. Energy efficiency in SME is monitored .

4) Institutional capacities of the state are strengthened with strengthening of state designated agency –SDA and contribution to state energy conservation fund –SECF- scheme .

5) School education programs are introduced to create awareness about energy efficiency through energy clubs !

6) Human resource development is being carried out by providing energy efficiency support instruments and related trainings.

7) Under the National action plan on climate change (NAPCC) , the national mission for enhanced energy efficiency (NMEEE) is started to strengthen the market for energy efficiency ! Under market transformation for energy efficiency –MTEE – two programs are developed which are Bachat Lamp Yojna – BLY and Super-efficient equipment programme – SEEP !

The central government may issue energy saving certificate to the designated consumer whose energy consumption is less than the prescribed norm !

It may be any corporate organization or it can be a proprietorship , need of the energy is basic business need and organization in today's age need to carry out full scale energy audits to note the exact status of their energy consumption in day to day operations and to find out if there are any energy losses which directly or indirectly accounts to huge business losses in overall accounting of business turnovers ! Energy audits can be carried out by three ways , one is walk through energy audit , second is target energy audit and third is detailed energy audit ! In fact , energy conservation inside organization and energy conservation because of firms manufactured products is best indicator of good practices of corporate governance in energy section of the business processes !

(*Ref: indiacode.nic.in & powermin.gov.in*)

45) Food Safety and Standards Act , 2006

It's an act to consolidate the laws relating to food and to establish the food safety and standards authority of India for laying down science based standards.

Being a highly populous country, India's food market is considerably big. The current size of the Indian food market is about 963.60 Billion

USD in 2023! The Indian food market is expected to grow every year by CAGR 7.23 % till 2028!

The prime food segments consist of Baby food, Bread and cereal products, confectionary and snacks, convenience food, dairy products and eggs, fish and sea food, fruits and nuts, meat, oil & fats, pet food, sauces and spices, spreads and sweeteners, vegetables.

(Ref:fssai.gov.in & statistics.com)

46) Indian Regulatory approach towards artificial intelligence, machine learning and industrial automation.

Artificial Intelligence, Machine learning, Industrial automation, Robotics are going to be the new employment sectors of future generations. Still, once these sectors will start their operation in industrial and non-industrial environments, the chances of human employment are going to affect! As far as legality of these innovations are concerned, there is a need to regulate the developments happening so far!

Currently there are no specific laws in India with regard to regulating AI, ML. Ministry of Electronics and Information Technology, the executive agency for AI related strategies, recently constituted four committees to bring in policy framework for AI.

The NITI Aayog has developed a set of seven responsible AI principles. These principles include safety & dependability, equality, inclusivity and non-discrimination, privacy and security, transparency, accountability and the protection and reinforcement of positive human values!

The Indian Industrial Automation market was valued at 10.72 Billion USD in 2021 and it is expected to reach USD 23.09 Billion by 2027 at CAGR 14.26 % as per business forecast!

Some of the industries where AI will show its application and influence are – Healthcare, Manufacturing, Cyber security, Transportation, Retail, Construction, Supply chain management, Business intelligence, Information technology, Education!

Major AI jobs has following roles – Machine learning Engineer, Robotics Engineer, Computer vision Engineer, Data scientist!

Considering the overall span of the artificial intelligence concept, a legal framework protecting the business interest of every sector and providing helpful service to AI client is at most important! On a larger scale, AI handles crucial data and makes decisions. Software programmes need to be written with due understanding of seven principles suggested by Niti Aayog!

(Ref: niti.gov.in & researchandmarkets.com)

47) Low Technology Industry

Industry that uses minimal technology to create new products which can affect current servicing industries to large extent is known as low technology industry! Also, the industry which uses simple tools and technique for creation of final product can be called as low technology industry. Textile, carpentry, black smithy, milling, food preservation skills like smoking-salting- pickling – drying, masonry work!

Labor intensive handicraft industry also uses human skill with low technology. **Handicrafts (Quality Control) Act, 1978** is made for improvement of quality of Handicrafts of Jammu and Kashmir so far as regards to their production. Indian Handicraft Industry is a lucrative export market. In the year 2021-22, the total export of handicraft industry was around 4.35 Billions!

India hosts around 744 handicrafts clusters employing nearly 2, 12,000 artisan and offers 35,000 products. Surat, Bareilly, Varanasi, Agra, Hyderabad, Lucknow, Chennai and Mumbai are few major clusters!

Examples of low tech industry also include building of solar oven, building of Eco-friendly house, living a low technology lifestyle where you use products that are created with simple technologies! They serve the same purpose but at minimal use of technology!

(Ref: Low technology, Wikipedia)

48) Bamboo Paper Industry (Protection) Act , 1925

This is an act to provide for the fostering and development of the Bamboo paper industry in British India!

Indian Paper and Pulp market is valued around 11.48 Billion USD. By 2029, it is expected to reach around 31.41 Billions!

Indian paper industry largely depends on rural agro industry. Around 12, 00,000 hectares of land is used for pulpwood production which is used in paper production.

Bamboo, Eucalyptus, Subabul trees are used for paper production in India!

Indian paper and pulp industry directly and indirectly provides employment to nearly 2.5 million people. In the last decade, Indian Paper and pulp industry reached up to 5th global rank.

(Ref: indiacode.nic.in & papermart.in)

49) The Merchant Shipping Act 1958

It's a comprehensive legislation dealing with merchant shipping in India! The statute had been enacted to foster the development and ensure the efficient maintenance of an Indian mercantile marine ecosystem in a manner best suited to serve the national interests.

(*Ref: dgshipping.gov.in*)

The Major Port Trust Act, 1963

It's an act to make provision for the constitution of port authorities for certain major ports in India and to vest the administration, control and management of such ports in such authorities and for matters connected therewith!

India host 13 major ports and 205 notified minor and intermediate ports. Approximately 95 % country's trade by volume and around 70% trade by value moves through maritime transport.

India is one of the top 5 ship recycling country. India holds 30% share in global ship recycling market. India hosts four major ship builder located in Vishakhapatnam, Kochi, Mumbai and Kolkata!

(Ref : tariffauthority.gov.in & iimidr.ac.in)

50) TRAI Act , 1997

This is an act to provide for the establishment of the Telecom Regulatory Authority of India and the Telecom Disputes Settlement and Appellate Tribunal to regulate the telecommunication services, adjudicate disputes, dispose of appeals and to protect the interest of service providers and consumers of the telecom sector, to promote and ensure orderly growth of the telecom sector and for matters connected therewith or incidental thereto.

India is the world's second largest telecommunication market with a subscriber base of 1.16 billion and has shown strong growth in last decade!

Out of total FDI in India, telecommunication sector is third largest sector which attracts 6.24 % of FDI flow. The 5G spectrum auction for deployment of 5G services are launched in 2022 with auction value 18.77 Billion USD.

Currently there are 5 major telecom operators serving the nation namely Bharati Airtel, MTNL, Vodafone Idea, Reliance Jio, BSNL.

(Ref: trai.gov.in & pib.gov.in)

51) The Water Act (Prevention & Control of pollution) 1974

This act was enacted by the central government in exercise of the power vested in it by resolutions passed by two or more state legislatures in accordance with article 252 of the constitution. The act establishes central board for the prevention and control of water pollution, describing its legal status, membership, functions and powers.

India, being an agri dependent nation employs various irrigation systems for supply of water for farms. The Indian irrigation market is projected to grow with CAGR of 10.9%

The current bottled water market size is 5.73 billion USD in 2023. The total Indian water market is estimated to about 14 Million USD with a growth rate of about 18% per year!

Indian water and waste water management industry has huge business potential because percentage of waste water treatment gives more scope for this business. Currently around 70 ambitious waste water treatment projects are being started in 20 cities of India!

(Ref:cpcb.nic.in & spml.co.in)

Indian Corporate Laws for Service Industries

1)   Intellectual Property Act

Intellectual property rights (IPR) refers to the legal rights given to the inventor or creator to protect his invention or creation for a certain period of time.

In India, there are seven types of intellectual property rights which are – copyright, trademarks, patents, geographical indications, plant varieties, industrial designs and semiconductor integrated circuit layout designs.

Industries that needs IPR includes creative services like advertising, fashion, floral , education industry , entertainment industry like film, music, video game , insurance industry for specific plans and products providing protection cover ,healthcare industry for IPR of specific surgeries , technology or invention , hospitality industry for protection of specific recipe's , mass media industry for protection of publication rights through broadcasting, news, internet , professional services which uphold certain technical skill which needs copyright protection , real estate industry for protection of their project designs, software industry for protection of software's !

Now apart from intellectual property protection of these service sectors, let's see one by one the specific acts that govern these service sectors.

(*Ref: ipindia.gov.in*)

2) Advertisement Act of 1951

An act to control the advertisement of drugs in certain cases, to prohibit the advertisement for certain purposes of remedies alleged to possess magic qualities and to provide for matters connected therewith.

Also deceptive and misleading advertisements are restricted under various legislation including the consumer protection Act, 1986, the cable television network rules 1994, the norms for journalist conduct issued by the press council of India Act and ASCI – Advertising standard council of India code!

The Indian advertising market is poised to expand 12.6 Billion with expected CAGR 14.7 % in 2023! In 2011, around 50 digital marketing agencies were there, now the number is reached to 1000 in 2023! India is also considered as worlds third best market for creative agencies as there are only 700 creative agencies in the nation with average ratio of 0.2 per 1,00,000 citizens !

The type of advertisement includes television advertising, print advertising, radio advertising, direct mail advertising, mobile advertising, display advertising, outdoor advertising, and social media advertising!

Advertisement industry as a service industry employs around 37,400 employees in India!

(Ref: indiacode.nic.in & economictimes.com)

3) Indecent representation of women (Prohibition) Act, 1986

An act to prohibit indecent representation of women through advertisements or in publications, writings, paintings, figures or in any other manner !

Indian Fashion industry projected to reach 19.86 Billion in 2023 ! Revenue in apparel market amount to 96.47 Billion USD in which women's apparel market volume is 43.65 Billion USD .

77.7 % of fashion models are women and 22.3% of fashion models are men ! Around 2400 modeling jobs were available in 2021 !

(Ref:wcd.nic.in & statista.com)

4) Bombay Prohibition Act ,1949

As per the Bombay prohibition act ,1949 , a tribal in schedule areas cannot store more than 25 Kg mahua flowers at a time . Mahua flowers are used in production of liquor .

Floriculture industry in one of the important industry according to cultural aspects of Indian Society ! The agricultural and processed food products export development authority (APEDA) was established by the Government of India under the agricultural and processed food products export development authority act passed by parliament in December , 1985 !

The Indian floriculture market size reached 231.7 Billion USD in 2022. It is expected to reach around 460 Billion USD by 2028 with CAGR of 12.13 % from 2022-2028 ! Floriculture also known as flower farming refers to the cultivation of flowering and ornamental plants !

(Ref:maharashtra.gov.in &
Researchandmarkets.gov.in)

5) Culture Industry & Protection of Human Rights 1993

This is an act to provide for the constitution of a National Human Rights commission, State Human Rights commissions and Human Right Courts for better protection of human rights and for matters connected therewith or incidental thereto.

Human rights means person belonging to certain culture, certain religion, certain race and certain linguistic background can enjoy their culture, they can declare their religion and practice it, and they can use the language in the community with other people of that background.

Cultural industries include film, television, radio, music, books and press! While creative industries covers advertising, design and architecture!

(*Ref: mha.gov.in*)

6) Education Industry & Right to Education

The constitution (Eighty Sixth Amendment) Act, 2002 inserted article 21-A in the constitution of India to provide free and compulsory education of all children in the age group of six to fourteen years as a fundamental right in such a manner as the state may, by law determine.

Being a populous country known for ancient knowledge reservoir, India has 10,22,386 government school, 82480 government aided schools and 3, 35,844 private schools!

The market size of Indian Education Industry was about 117 Billion USD across India .This market is expected to rise up to 225 Billion USD by financial year 2025 in the country. 3 Crore people comprising Teaching, Non-Teaching and support staff is employed in Education Industry. This translates into 12-15 crore people's livelihood in the nation. This makes Education Industry as one of the top 5 employment generators in the country.

(Ref: education.gov.in & ezyschooling.com)

7) The Prasar Bharati (Broadcasting corporation of India) Act , 1990

Broadcasting Corporation, to be known as Prasar Bharati and define its composition, functions and powers. The act grants autonomy to All India Radio and to Doordarshan!

(*Ref: indiacode.nic.in*)

The Cable Television networks act, 1995

This is an act to regulate the operation of cable television networks in the country and for matters connected therewith or incidental thereto.

In India , the digital media segment grew 29% to reach 5.2 Billion USD in 2021 , online gaming grew 28% in 2021 to reach 1.2 Billion USD and is expected to reach 1.9 Billion USD by 2024, the filmed entertainment segment grew 28% in 2021, 757 films released out of which 100 films directly released on streaming platforms .

(*Ref:indiacode.nic.in & ibef.org*)

8) The Insurance Regulatory Development Authority Act 1999

An act to provide for the establishment of an Authority to protect the interests of holders of insurance policies , to regulate, promote and ensure orderly growth of the insurance industry and for matters connected therewith or incidental thereto and further to amend the insurance act 1938 , the life insurance corporation act ,1956 and the general insurance business (Nationalization) Act, 1972.

Insurance industry is growing and to protect from life risks and business risks , people are preferring to pay insurance premium and get a certain proportionate sum after maturity of policy !

In the financial year 2020-2021 , the Life Insurance Sector in India posted a gross premium amount of roughly INR 5.73 trillion – approx. 81.3 Billion USD which shows 12.75 % increase over the prior year , with private insurers accounting for around 33.7 % of overall premium insured by the industry .

(Ref:thc.nic.in & securenow.in)

9) The Epidemic Diseases Act , 1897

This is an act to provide for the better prevention of the spread of Dangerous Epidemic diseases .

(Ref : indiacode.nic.in)

Transplantation of Human organ and tissues act ,2014

This act is made for transplantation of human organs and tissues . Several organs can be donated after death of a person as per his or her wish post natural death or complications like brain stem death .

(Ref : mohfw.gov.in)

Tobacco control act 2003

An act to prohibit the advertisement of and to provide for the regulation of trade and commerce in , and production , supply and distribution of cigarettes and other tobacco products and for matters connected therewith or incidental thereto .

Indian health care sector is a wide spread network of hospitals , clinics , pharmacies , service centers and trauma care units . In India , health sector has several disciplines like allopathy, homeopathy, aurved , unani ! Accordingly trained professional provide their service to mankind !

Healthcare Industry in India is projected to reach 372 billion USD by 2022 . Healthcare industry in India comprises of hospitals, medical devices, clinical trials, outsourcing, telemedicine, medical tourism, health insurance and medical equipment.

NHWA – National Health Workforce Accounts study reveals that there are 5.76 million health workers are present in India which include allopathic doctors – 1.16 million,nurses (midvives) -2.34 million, pharmacist – 1.20 million , dentist – 0.27 million and traditional medical practitioner – 0.79 million !

To support healthcare services India has total of more than 600 medical colleges which offer seat for MBBS /BDS which are recognized by medical council of India !   India has 542 medical colleges which teach MBBS , out of those 273 colleges are government colleges !

(*Ref : mohfw.gov.in*)

10)   Laws related to hospitality industry

Hotel industry in one of the important service industry and it caters to the need of many professionals who are traveling for work related assignments as well as general citizens who are travelling for tourism purpose .

Hospitality law are related to establishment of hotels and permissions required for set up , hospitality laws are related to various contracts of services –such as payment to workers and service providers , security of customers , type of services to be included in service package, various taxes and their liability , hospitality laws also related to overall environmental care and food hygiene .

Some of the Hotel industry permissions requirements are –

1) Building completion certificate
2) Occupancy certificate
3) Shop and act certificate
4) Water act & Air act certificate
5) Municipal corporation certificate
6) Employee state insurance act
7) Apprenticeship act
8) Eating and lodging license
9) Eating house license,
10) Board signage and Neon sign license
11) License for limited money exchange
12) Factory licenses for the laundry purposes
13) Mild liquor license
14) Bar license
15) Public performance license
16) Cold storage license
17) FSSAI license
18) License for chimney under smoke nuisance act
19) Permits for taxis under motor vehicle act
20) License for boilers & generators, mixers and grinders
21) NOC from fire department .

Size of the Indian hotel industry is about 7.66 billion USD in 2023 and same is projected to reach around 10.53 billion USD in 2027. Almost

61.33 million users are expected to come by 2027 ! As of May 2022 , India hosts 1377 classified hotel as star hotels ! There are 579 three star hotel predominantly . 259 four star with alcohol and 166 four star without alcohol . Five star deluxe hotels numbers is 149 while five star with alcohol numbers is 135. Five stars Without alcohol consist of 52 . There are 26 two star and 11 one star hotel .

(*Ref: ipleaders.in*)

11)   Information services sector

The size of Indian IT & Business process management industry is estimated to 227 Billion USD in 2022. The domestic revenue is around 49 Billion USD while export revenue is 181 Billion USD . There are more than 1,70,000 IT companies in India ! As of March 2022 , around 5 million people are employed in Indian IT sector ! There is IT act 2000 which we have seen earlier . Apart from that, there are several permissions and supporting provisions are required to set an information services industry . Some of the necessary compliances are –

1) Permanent Account Number
2) Tax deduction and collection account number
3) Minimum wages
4) Goods and service tax
5) Professional Tax
6) Employee state insurance
7) Employee provident fund

Apart from this , there are several statutory compliances are required to run an IT industry . The relevant acts are –

1) The workmen compensation act 1923
2) The trade unions act ,1926
3) The payment of wages act , 1936
4) The industrial employment standing orders act ,1946
5) The industrial disputes act , 1946
6) The employees state insurance act , 1948
7) The minimum wages act , 1948
8) The factories act , 1948
9) The apprentice act , 1961
10) The payment of bonus act , 1965

11) The contract labor act (Regulation and Abolition) ,1970
12) The payment of gratuity act , 1972
13) The equal remuneration act , 1976
14) Interstate migrant workmen act ,1979 (Regulation of employment and conditions of service)
15) The child labor (Prohibition and Regulation act) ,1986

Being a service industry , an extremely favorable future is predicted globally !

(*Ref: ibef.org*)

12)   Leisure Industry :

Leisure industry including sport is a booming industry now days . Promotion of sports brings people together , it inspires people to win and it keeps them healthy ! Apart from this , there is award money and commercial benefits as a sportsman !

There is no sport legislation as such but various agreements in sport and disciplinary actions in sports are taken with some set rules by sport bodies and sport authorities .

Some well-known sport rules are :

1) Contracts between sports players and other parties .
2) Doping Policies .
3) Harassment in sports .
4) Sports injuries regarding the liability .
5) Tort law
6) Broadcasting rights
7) Conflict of interest regarding the endorsement by the players.
8) Endorsement and advertising .
9) Intellectual property rights .
10) Player's rights .

Some of the sport authorities are :

1) Ministry of youth affair and sports.
2) National sports federation
3) Sports law and welfare association of India .
4) Sports authority of India.
5) Team Authorities like BCCI and Hockey Federation .

Indian sport industry has several business segments like sport media , broadcasting , sport apparel , sport kits , sport ground complex !

The Indian sport apparel market was worth USD 579.47 million in 2021.

Total revenue in sports segment is projected to reach US dollar 5.11 million in 2022.

The market size , measured by revenue ,of the sport franchises industry is 39.6 Billion dollars in 2023 !

Sport & recreational activity industry employment is observing growth from a period between 2000 to 2019 . In 2020, it dropped and now in 2023 it is expected to grow till the level of 1,33,900 by 2024 !

(*Ref : Sports in India , statista.com , Wikipedia*)

13) Mass media industry .

Mass media industry consists of many segments which start from broadcasting , news media , publishing , entertainment , internet .

We have seen , these respective industries earlier with respect to their relevant laws .

Internet is proven as an international streaming platform since last ten years . Now days most of the services are available on the internet and one can get the necessary details before purchasing a particular service . With 780 million internet users in the nation , Indian internet industry is supposed to reach a valuation equal to 5 trillion by 2030. The ICT – Internet and communication technology and digital economy are contributing 13 percent to national GDP ! An average Indian spends around 7.3 hours on their smart phones , this is one of the biggest digital consumption rates . Short video commerce is widely accepted and people are investing their time and talent to make it employable deal ! Around 50,000 professional creators are there who use their skills to broadcast digital content on the internet !

(Ref: mass media, Wikipedia)

14) Professional services industry

There are some professional services which earns money by providing their scientific knowledge . These professional services include accountants – CA's , Doctors , Lawyers, Engineers, Architects ! The laws and rules of these professional services are governed by their respective working domain . These professionals can set their own business, they can start their own design agency , they can find long term employment in relevant industry or they can open consulting firm ! Once degree is attained , they can use that knowledge to make financial earnings.

There are around 90,000 registered architects for a population of almost 1.38 billion !

There are around 3.51 lakh registered chartered accounts in India and around 7,50,000 students enrolled for the course !

More than 15 lakhs engineers take their degree per year India !

There are 13,08,009 registered allopathy doctors in India by 2022 !

There are 1.4 Million enrolled advocates in India !

(*Ref : Professional services, Wikipedia*)

15)   Retail Industry

Indian retail industry is a huge one and for serving 1.38 billion people , there are number of retail outlets, shopping malls and shopping festivals throughout the year !

The laws related to retail industry are related with various licenses to open the shops and retail centers, safety rules, storage facilities rules , packaging rules .

Systematic tax laws are made for tax calculation . Retail business is mostly cash turnover business. Customers directly purchase items they need and pay the bill on direct counters !

There is no manufacturing is being carried out . The major portion of the work consists of buying items either from factory or from wholesale sellers and selling it to retain customers with a certain profit margin.

India's retail sector is worth USD 836 billion in which 81.5 % contribution comes from traditional return . India has around 12 million retail outlets , a million wholesalers and distributors ! India has now total mall stock of 92.9 million square feet spread across 271 operational malls in eight top markets ! More than 35 million people are employed in retail industry ! ✹✹✹

(Ref: ibef.org & indiatimes.com)

CHAPTER 18 : BOARD'S MESSAGE

" Our proven technical skills coupled with this firm's upgraded technological advancement will open more avenues of bilateral growth in highly anticipated growing market! "

Image Courtesy: Evangeline Shaw, Unsplash.com

18.1 Introduction:

In the last chapter, we have seen some of the widely used labor laws and corporate governance framework for different sectors of the industrial societies! Laws governs masses and ways of functioning ,so much so that , having a right law in place signifies that people are concerned about ethical ways of doing the business activities !

Every corporate house has a central policy making system which is headed by respective board of directors! This body is a body of appointed members by the promoters of the corporate house! Technical, management, leadership expert from respective walks of the society are appointed in the director's chair which is headed by sole or joint owner of the corporate house which can be a professionally managed firm or it can be a traditional business unit!

Chief Director can be supported by one or more co-directors to take care of different business functions and divisions! Suppose in an organization, there are five different units

Catering to five different technical needs of customers, then each field expert will take charge as director of respective unit having specialization of that domain and he or she will continue to look after the management team working with that respective unit which can be formed of respective group heads, line managers, engineers, technicians, designers! The system of result reporting will make flow of communication from top to bottom, bottom to top and across various functional units! The key permissions to allow a certain capex transaction will be done after review of respective unit's director endorsed by chief director! Hence, knowing the role of every director is critical in understanding the efficient functioning of corporate governance! In this chapter, we are going to see various sample directors message, in different business scenarios which will help to understand the long term and short term vision of a business leader! Director's message is an inspirational sharing which coaches the people working daily with the organization! These messages are assurances that whatever may be the business situation; organization will work hard to grow!

18.2 Directors Message – Collaboration

Hello Team,

This gives us immense pleasure in announcing recent technological collaboration with market leader in this domain! Our proven technical skills coupled with this firm's upgraded technological advancement will open more avenues of bilateral growth in highly anticipated growing market! We thank each one of you for extending your best service in all forms of regular functioning! We wish you all the best!

18.3 Directors Message – Acquiring new market

Hi All,

What a day this is! We all have thrived to make this day happen! After ten years of continuous struggle in the domain, finally we have set our first offshore business unit capable of designing, manufacturing and servicing our key product in foreign territory adhering to their national manufacturing standards and quality norms!

This business development will provide us opportunities to serve north part of the export market to more than 50% and by which in coming ten years , we will become market leader by having market penetration more than 80% ! So, cheers for this achievement! As a part of celebration, we are giving a special allowance to all team members in coming festive season! Thanks a lot!

18.4 Directors Message – Declaring dividend

Good Evening Friends,

This year was a yet another fruitful year for all of our business functions both technically and commercially! This year we rose up our current share capital by 12 % more and added to kitty of business profit after tax, depreciation equal to nearly 15 % higher to last YTD! As a result of same, we are happy to announce a bonus of 2% on maximum face value of last YTD share prices as gesture of business goodwill! This year the order scenario is positive and we will make this year even more fruitful by consolidating the business momentum we achieved this year!

18.5 Directors Message – Setting up new Research & Development Facility with mega investment plan

Good Morning All,

With this message, we are very very happy to share with you that to assist recent technological breakthrough and in a direction to promote the research culture across the firm, we are setting up a new research and development unit in our mother plant! We are investing heavily and planning to yield at least one new product per month to serve various customers of our society! A business prospers when Research and development blooms! So, make this place a good exchange place of wisdom and creativity and let's do something highly effective and useful for the society! Our best wishes for your continued association! Your all suggestions and queries will be addressed once the formal opening of this unit takes place! Thanks!

18.6 Directors Message – About New Trade Union Contract

Namaste Everyone,

It gives us immense pride and pleasure in signing the new contract with trade union about the new compensation structure, facilities and job commitments! Currently business scenario is much positive, many countries are keen to invest in our ecosystem and hence this is the time to deliver as per expectations! The three year contract will add Rs 21,000 per month in the basic through intervals of 7000 Rs per year! Apart from this, host of new employee facilities will be made available by registering and booking on facility application. Everything will be made available at the point of fingure tip! This contract is carefully drafted for all round welfare and health improvement of every family member attached to our organization. Considering current challenging climate conditions, an enhanced mediclaim plan and seven days paid sick leaves is an added perk of this new contract from organizations point of view. We hope, you extend your full-fledged co-operation and maintain the brand recognition!

18.7 Directors Message – Launching cost saving six sigma lean management growth drive

Hello Team,

Good morning and greetings!

Recently the sales and marketing teams of various functional divisions came together to find out the various differences in costing of our products and services and they jointly derived a fact that lot of work can be done through use of six sigma lean management technique to reduce segmental costing and overall profit margin !

As per this validated feedback from their side to the board of directors, we are launching organization wide six sigma lean management drive to make our processes more compliant to six sigma norms. Our basic purpose will be focused on reducing various system wastes and making system DMAICS compliant! We will take a simple challenge in our hand and will try to analyze till it provide us desired cost saving solution. It is estimated that, if we all follow this technique, we could save to more than 15% of last year's total turnover! These saving will directly get added to our bottom line by which everyone will get increased rise and performance incentives for sure! So, be prepared to give your best in each process and perform more and more projects by using six sigma lean management methodologies!

18.8 Directors Message – Grand opening of seven holiday homes!

Dear All,

As a part of consolidating our commitment to work –life balance, we are opening seven holiday homes with all ultra-modern facilities and very very comfortable charges! These holiday homes are located in little bit distant landscapes near the famous tourist attractions and we are tied up with renowned tour operators and hospitality brand to take care of all travel and staying necessities! Organizations mobile friendly application will take care of booking of every employee! We are providing option of booking at seven holiday homes each is having arrangement of 50 fully furnished rooms. The facility will remain open throughout the year!

The maximum stay allowed is 30 days without any special permission if you have necessary earned leaves! Hope, you all enjoy this facility and return with excellent freshness to deal with daily innovation in the respective fields! Thank you!

18.9 Directors Message – Felicitation of super annuation batch!

Dear All,

Since the launch of our business operations 40 years back, this year, the first batch of 100 employees' is getting super annuated this year! That year, we recruited 300 people, out of which these 100 people has served for organization sincerely and with complete dedication to their respective jobs!

In the initial challenges of setting the organizations functional streams, these people worked creatively to establish a strong foundation of operational excellence and caring values which are useful for business turnover!

In this event, we are celebrating the first batch of superannuation and wishing them best for their future endvaours! Thanks!

18.10 Directors Message – Challenging times and implementation plan

Dear All,

Good morning and greetings of the season!

As per recent news, it's going to be little bit tough for businesses to continue their journey! Having our strong customer driven performance culture we are implementing a sustainability plan that will take care of such business environment! With this plan, our dedicated officers will directly interact with prospective customers about their requirements and immediately within three days' time will make it clear to customer that the feasible business solutions are available and they can go ahead in commercial discussions! Our design team has given idea of this mission and they have committed to extend their contribution! Best wishes to everyone! ⊛⊛⊛

CHAPTER 19 : INTERNATIONAL BRANDING

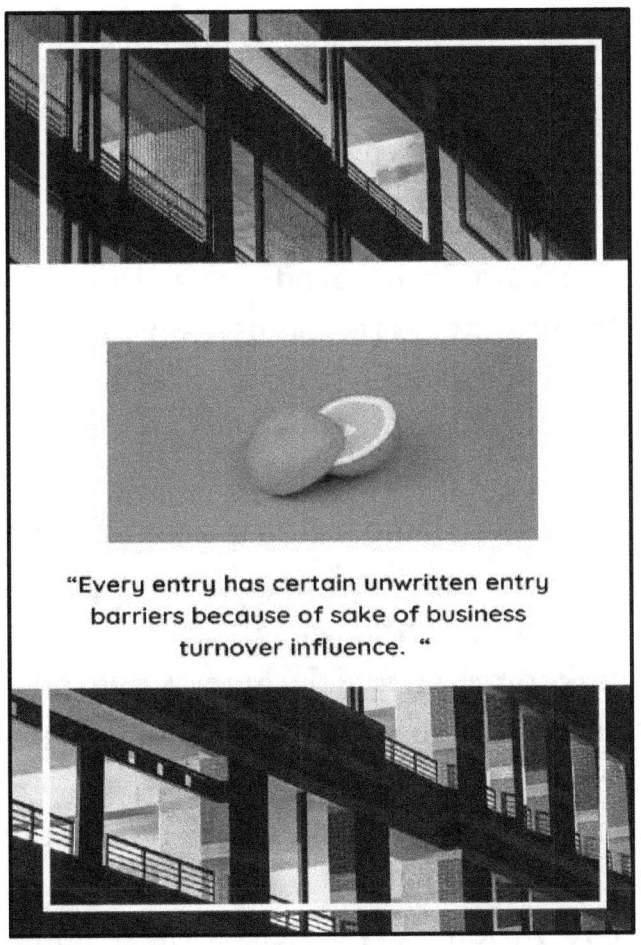

"Every entry has certain unwritten entry barriers because of sake of business turnover influence."

Image Courtesy: Davisuko, Unsplash.com

19.1 Introduction:

Looking at the corporate governance with open eyes is a useful exercise for business owners! Corporate business is all about meeting international needs at best available quality standards and by adhering to tighter delivery schedules! In international market, cost is not that much a concern, since delivery of supply is a critical aspect and people generally import material or services which cannot be produced locally or cannot be produced within available time frame. Always remember, any procurement search always begins from nearest supplier and ceases with a supply chain solution from farthest supplier! As a result, the nearest supply exhibit faster delivery, comparative pricing as they have to compete with local competitors and fastest delivery since supply is in local circles within certain kilometers which can be travelled in one or two hour maximum! Intermediate product and service supply is little bit costly as it adds up to transport cost , various safety insurances , duties and taxes as well as risk of transportation through various urgencies, strikes and other sudden reasons ! The overseas supply are far more expensive as they involve shipping charges

, freight charges , transit insurances , LD charges , custom duties and other taxes ! They need maximum time out of three ways of deliveries – local, intermediate and overseas! The other big challenge associated with imported supply is its availability in international market! Internationally available products are exchanged in foreign currencies and currency rates keep changing on regular interval. So one has to be very much updated about the price hike or price fall before booking and after booking! A pure business sense of dealing in international market give rise to maximum profit saving and less expenses on procurement! International credit system can be tighter, so one has to meet required safety deposit and other financial assets before entering into procurement transactions!

19.2 Why International Branding is essential?

According to just explained need of material and service delivery, having international branding of product and services is essential to reach remote market and book good amount of profit. In any industrial scenario, the extent to which you serve export customer or overseas customers decides your speed of growth. Export profit margin is always higher than domestic profit margin. One thing, you are supplying resources which are scarce at their end. Second thing, in domestic trade, the focus of supplying product is to serve the nation through technological advances! So, to attract more and more overseas customers, we require international branding!

19.3 Dimensions of International Branding

Let's see, how the different dimensions of international branding are featured in products and services created to understand the path of supply and after sales services.

A) International Manufacturing standards

If you want to sell your products in international market, then you have to manufacture these products according to international practices which are explained in international standards, specifications and codes. International standards are accepted over major portion of the globe and different country or continents prefer certain manufacturing standards based on their user experience in particular service environment. As a manufacturer, you have to take care that while manufacturing the product in your country, the service conditions should be met properly. With respect to which you have to confirm minimum design metal temperature, its other performance parameters! If a readymade product is available with you, which meets your export need, you can directly divert that product to overseas customer by doing necessary small modifications without altering the core product! When your business reaches a certain age, you are always on a drive to explore overseas market! In earlier times, sales and marketing executives used to travel across various continents to participate in trade shows, industrial seminars and other networking event by which they used to get information about new developments and necessary need of their products. They used to have a talk with concern parties and they used to introduce themselves through trade associate or through self-introduction! Business used to happen after detailed formal discussion and commercial know-how! In today's digital era, lots of things are happening over a video call or a video conference where people from different locations can participate and can discuss opportunities of sales and marketing!

B) <u>International Quality, Manufacturing and Services system</u>

When you are manufacturing products according to international codes, your infrastructure also need to fulfill the criteria suggested in system of standards. You need to invest heavily in building world class manufacturing facilities capable of installing high end machines, high grade raw material, trained professionals and above all a quickest surveillance to catch in process happenings! The product has to test at various intervals to avoid any rejection during finish stage. Even after sales of product, manufacturer has to bear the warranty period and make sure that products manufactured don't get failed in that period! Certification plays important role in international branding and when your facility is equipped with certain international certification, your chances of getting international customers increases!

C) International market presence

One of the important aspects of international branding is your registration in international trade offices! Various countries has trade associations and sales network. If you want to get international business then you must enroll in these trade networks by fulfilling their entry requirements. Every entry has certain unwritten entry barriers because of sake of business turnover influence. Because of market dynamics, addition of a major player affects overall business momentum and hence every business owner has to take care of their business during entries of other players! The game of competition may become tougher if the new player has huge investment potential!

D) International Events

International events are part of larger involvement of many participants. Here, all participants get a booth to display their products and introduce them to many visitors. For sake of excellence, you may introduce your products through audio-visual presentation, making advertisements or by showcasing live demonstrations! The mobile, LED, Video games – all these products were part of trade exhibitions before they commercially traded everywhere! See, the trade exhibitions catch the response of industry experts and allow them to comment about their user experience! When your product receives classic rating, same rating is marketed when your product is ready for sale! International events have high reputation and every journalist tries to catch the event highlights! So, getting good marks in such event is equivalent to brand success later!

E) Brand Advertising

Advertising is known as one of important art and science of selling your product in huge amount! Advertisements are generally limited times creative conversations that describe the product in easy to understand way and make a customer ready to buy the product! Advertisements always insist buyers to buy those products, however they don't sell product actually! Decision of buying product is totally belongs to customer and hence he can research other options before making a final deal!

International advertisements can be broadcasted on several platforms such as television, cinema halls, internet, radio, print mediums like newspaper and magazines! The whole aim of this type of branding is to make the viewer conversant with brand and its applications!

People love to see decorations and artistic work. Advertisements always make good use of communication skills when they impart technical features of the products being advertised. A dire need of why the product to be procured is clearly indicated in advertisement!

F) <u>Cycles of International Trades</u>

When a new business gets international listing and initial sales, the first task is to supply the first order correctly and accurately. Your first order gives you all necessary experience to supply the product according to client need. Here you get all the details through purchase enquiry and later fulfills those through product completion. When you complete your product, you provide a completion certificate in the form of manufacturers test certificate which speaks about adhering committed clauses of supply!

In second supply, you repeat the process and observe the results. When client find the supply in correct condition, he gives clearance and thus you get know-how of supplying product to certain overseas region!

When you met with certain delivery challenges, all it required is to have a logical dialogue with approving authority about product features and relevant facts at your end! Once you clarify and resolve their doubts, the product gets accepted and you get final payment at your end!

G) <u>Return and Replacements</u>

As a part of international supply, you have to always take care of belief of customer. The brand identity is nothing but retained trust level of customer irrespective of business variations. Brand loyalty is one of the important trade aspect and every producer try to grow brand loyalty of customer towards their products or services!

When an international supply found to be a defective one, you have to take care of the observation, find the details at your end and commit to correct the error if it belongs to supplier side. If the error belongs to customer side or transit side, then necessary dialogue is required to ascertain the ownership of error. Once the ownership is ascertained, you have to provide a replacement which can either be a free replacement or it can be paid replacement!

Following the best international practices of supply, corporate governance strengthen international trade relations and make their businesses prosper over a long time! Ultimately its journey of becoming a branded supplier!

CHAPTER 20 : FOREIGN EXCHANGE

" when your economy is strong, your exchange rates with respective countries are far better and international trade relations are also supportive to each other! "

Image Courtesy: Steve Johnson , Unsplash.com

20.1 Introduction

When Corporate Governance focus on finances especially trade in relation with foreign countries, corporates has to take care of one of the important reserves which is known as foreign exchange reserves or simply Forex! In this chapter, we are going to see various provisions with which one can avail the benefits of Forex for simplifying business transactions!

20.2 Reserves and Surplus

Managing business is all about creating products and services and balancing financial transactions. When these two things are handled properly, business start producing profit by selling those products to prospectus customer.

As we know there are two basic financial transactions every business encounters. These are debit transaction and credit transaction. Business also has to take care of return on investment, loan and interest, reserves and surplus, debentures, depreciation, profit and loss, taxes – both direct and indirect taxes!

In a financial year when EBITDA is attained, its net earnings from the business before paying taxes, interest on business loans if any, depreciation value of assets and amortization! When all these components are paid off as business liabilities, we get net profit from business! Over the year, business accumulates profit in this way and many business owners keep investing this profit as a capital in the business to help business grow!

It's the prudence of business fund manager to decide how the profit earned from business transactions is to be maximized in coming future! Many directors always follow the vision they laid out before starting the business and before crafting their annual business plan!

When business plan attains a certain planned financial goal, the relevant business decision is taken. With the help of that decision, next level of financial growth is achieved and this process of decision making based on actual financial results goes on continuous basis! The all aim of these business transactions is to make major funds available for business processes!

Reserves and surplus is the fund available with the organization at any time which can be highly liquid or can be moderately invested in various income creating resources! Means a reserve and surplus of 1000 Cr can be distributed in various forms – It can be deposited in bank, e.g. – 200 Cr, It can be invested in buying future real estate for business, such as 300 Cr land purchase for future operations, it can be invested in diversified business which is capable of generating per month profit of 10 Cr by using these remaining 500 Cr! Business owner can anytime remove this money from invested sources at a certain withdrawal charges!

Foreign exchange reserves are the business fund specifically allocated for business need where international transaction is applicable. When you have to carry out international procurement, you have to pay the bills through foreign exchange. The rates of foreign exchange keeps changing and you have to keep track of these changes continuously. As a result, you have to always keep a certain amount for reserves and surplus to meet the need of foreign exchange!

20.3 Forex Transactions

Banks and other Forex dealing authorized agencies act as mediator in between foreign exchange transactions happening between sellers and buyers. The concept of forex currency trading market and Forex exchange is different in many ways!

In Foreign Exchange, person or organization transfers equivalent amount of respective foreign currency with an applicable exchange service charge and get the foreign currency for necessary payments! The received foreign currency is credited to beneficiary account and procurement is done internationally!

In Forex Trading Market, people invest their money in number of foreign currencies and book their profits by selling those currencies when respective up or down in currency in noted! It means, if you are investing 5 Cr in USD, you will get equivalent USD as per that moments value. In future, if dollar appreciated, you can sell it and book a profit! If dollar is depreciated, you can further buy more dollars as a future investment. This way you earn profit in Forex

Trade market! Here decision of investment and removal lies with investor! Whereas, in Foreign Exchange process, you get equivalent currency in return of your national currency to simplify the business transaction.

As we have seen in the last chapter, Export Products are scarce resources for a purchaser. So seller always wants to have leverage on every purchase value. Basically, things which are exported have a huge demand, they are not easily available and they cannot be produced anywhere else! That's the reason, the country which produces export products; get excess money from business dealings. In demand – supply equilibrium, the purchaser always has to fulfill the requirements of seller if he wants to buy the product from him. If the seller is not reducing the prices and asking for higher value of foreign exchange, purchaser can search other available options!

So before every foreign exchange transaction, firm has to ensure, necessary funds for currency conversion are available. If the funds are not available then to carry on the purchase of goods they have to take loans and buy the material. When products are realized and sold, they can make the profit and can pay the loan!

20.4 Major Foreign Currencies

Here, we are going to see major foreign currencies and their equivalent Indian rupees as on 25 April, 2024

SR.NO	FOREIGN CURRENCY	INDIAN EXCHANGE
1	USD	81.92 INR
2	EURO	90.40 INR
3	POUND STERLING	102.20 INR
4	JAPANESE YEN	0.61 INR
5	AUSTRALIAN DOLLAR	54.61 INR
6	CANADIAN DOLLAR	60.38 INR

SR.NO	FOREIGN CURRENCY	INDIAN EXCHANGE
7	SWISS FRANC	92.41 INR
8	CHINESE YUAN	11.84 INR
9	HONG CONG DOLLAR	10.44 INR
10	NEW ZEALAND DOLLAR	50.55 INR
11	KUWAITI DINAR	267.62 INR
12	UAE DIRHAM	22.31 INR
13	OMANI RIYAL	212.78 INR
14	SAUDI RIYAL	21.84 INR
15	QATARI RIYAL	22.50 INR
16	MOROCCAN DIRHAM	8.12 INR
17	IRAQI DINAR	0.062 INR
18	EGYPTIAN POUND	2.65 INR

SR.NO	FOREIGN CURRENCY	INDIAN EXCHANGE
19	BAHRAINI DINAR	217.36 INR
20	ARGENTINE PESO	0.37 INR
21	COMBODIAN RIYAL	0.020 INR
22	JAMIACAN DOLLAR	0.54 INR
23	SINGAPORE DOLLAR	61.33 INR
24	SRILANKAN RUPEE	0.25 INR
25	RUSSIAN RUBLE	1.01 INR
26	MEXICAN PESO	4.56 INR
27	BELARUS RUBLE	32.59 INR
28	BANGLADESHI TAKA	0.78 INR
29	NEPALI RUPYA	0.63 INR
30	THAI BAHT	2.38 INR

It can be easily seen that foreign currency exchange rates completely depends upon the availability of critical natural resources , the technological advances inside a nation and overall population of the nation !

20.5 Business Decisions of Export Trade

When we have to start export trade with different nation the first requirement is government approval! Various National leaders and diplomatic officers visit each other's country to set the scene of international trade and corporate affairs. Who will do business with whom in global environment is decided with the help of free trade agreements! Various sanctions are taken in between two participating nations whenever they visit each other to observe the industrial scenario and to fulfill the need of the population!

India being the highly populous country and world's top 5 economies has remained always an attraction both for investors and also for international manufacturers! Products once designed for India and sold with appealing marketing strategies, get sold out! Once the product is liked, business momentum continues and it gives rise to boost in demand of the product!

Every Indian businessman first tries to fulfill the domestic need before they go ahead for export business!

20.6 What If Foreign Exchange is growing in negative direction?

This is one of the most difficult situations for any country because of various political and natural circumstances! In such situation when your economic condition is not healthy, you can buy very less material at high price which may not fulfill the required production demand! Because of shortage of money, deadlines will not be achieved and this will lead to reduced confidence of the customer!

In a positive situation, when your economy is strong, your exchange rates with respective countries are far better and international trade relations are also supportive to each other! Still there will be various international organizations which will try to set balance between various nations, but in the end when sales of critical resources is concerned; the decisions are taken by the nations who own those resources!

Business at international level gets excelled with appropriate balance of foreign exchange equations!

20.7 Best Practices of Maintaining Foreign Exchange Transactions

It's always a good habit to communicate your foreign exchange requirement in advance to finance manager so that he can study the trend and issue you required foreign exchange at best exchange price ! Prudential finance managers can buy foreign exchange in return of the domestic currency with the countries in which the transactions are regular. Over the period of few months, one gets an idea about the variation in currency and accordingly necessary purchase decisions are taken. E.g. a USD changes to following values in one week – 1 USD @ 80 INR, @ 81 INR, @ 81INR, @ 84 INR, @ 83 INR, @ 80 INR @ 78 INR! So, one can see the fluctuation in currency values, which is plus or minus 2/3 points! This much difference can be adjusted by procuring necessary foreign currency in advance!

20.8 Business effects of foreign exchange

Everyone wish to buy new raw material at lower foreign exchange price so that he can procure more in same price! e.g. Petrol barrel's purchased at 100 USD per barrel for 100 barrels account to transaction of 10000 USD! Suppose on same day, the foreign exchange value is 80 Rupees per USD, so one has to arrange funds equivalent to 80 x 10000 USD = 800000 INR! So, if you have 8 Lakhs ready with you, you can directly receive necessary currency and can procure the material! Now in second week , the barrel price is changed to 105 USD per barrel , now dollar to rupee exchange rate is same @ 80 Rs, now to purchase 200 barrels this time , you will require 105 x 200 = 21000 USD , so necessary rupees are 21000 x 80 = 16,80,000 ! So the difference in prices can be seen easily! This time for 100 barrels, you need 840000 INR which is 40,000 more than last week! Now, in third week, you need 300 barrels and cost of barrel is 120 USD per barrel and your exchange rate is 85 INR, then the transaction will be far more expensive than previous two! You need

120x 300 = 36000 USD @ 85 INR = 30, 60,000!

So, before initiating any international transaction, one has to go with stocking policy and bare minimum material requirement planning. Expert professionals keep close eye of material prices and they always keep searching new supplier who can reduce the raw material price!

Raw material price form almost 60-70 % costing of the finished product, hence procurement decisions forms important framework before meeting customer needs!

Few services are also imported! When a typical technical skill is not available, one can invite foreign delegate, pay their fees in foreign exchange value and get the benefit of required service!

Material planning is nothing but per unit requirement of certain material and number of such units to be completed in respective month! Accordingly gross requirement is given and as per priority of purchases, a fine tuning is done between the required material and purchased material! Received material is processed for production of finished products!

20.9 Role of Chief Finance Officer in handling foreign exchange

Finance is the fuel of business and chief finance officer has to play a leading and assisting role in business environment to manage funds constructively! He or She is the first person who decides whether to allow a certain financial transaction or not! Many times when business urgencies are there, he has to make funds available to chief executive officer for making technical decisions.

Chief Executive officer always analyses technical requirements, management strategies for delivering required goods in required time and assuring profit-loss account maintains healthy state throughout the year! He has to co-ordinate with marketing, sales, research, design, manufacturing, material, quality, service, maintenance, shipping, installation team effectively!

Chief finance officer assist chief executive officer to provide required funds and he also plays role of auditee when finance audit is carried out! Audit confirms accuracy of dealings that happened in the financial year! ⊛⊛⊛

CHAPTER 21 : SHARES & EQUITY

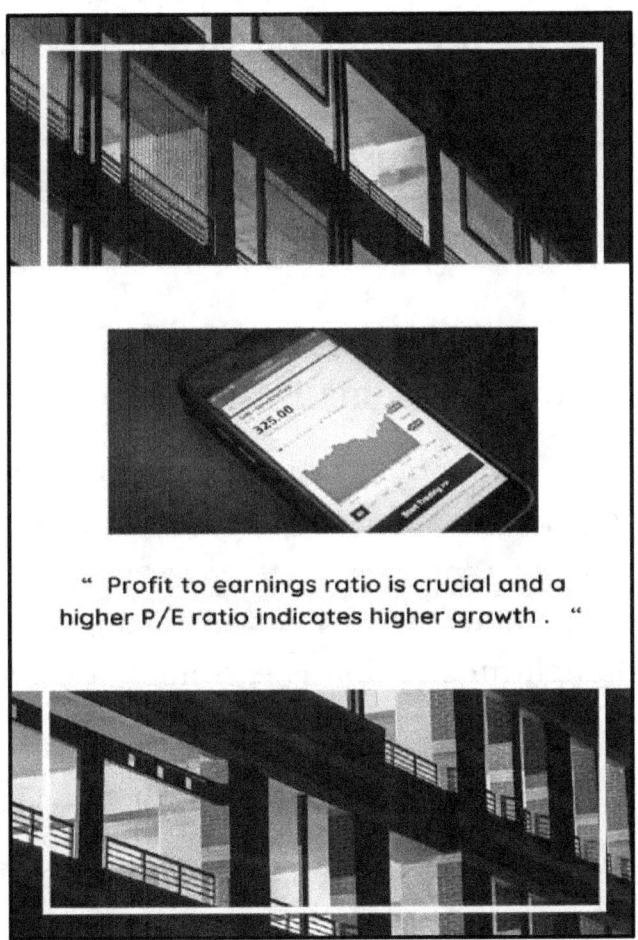

" Profit to earnings ratio is crucial and a higher P/E ratio indicates higher growth . "

Image Courtesy: Michael Fortsch, Unsplash.com

21.1 Introduction

Major part of this book is covered to explain important aspects of corporate governance and its effect on accelerating business momentum. Next ten chapter of this book will deal with various leadership and organization building aspects which are equally important, same as knowledge of financial terms. So, let's see the next chapter in row which discusses about shares & equity!

21.2 Capital Building Techniques

In any organizational set up, capital is hugely responsible to accelerate the business dynamics. When we say, the organization is vibrant and dynamic; it simply means the speed of thoughtful decision is extremely high so that all business operations get completed in agreed time. When the targets are achieved in time or they are achieved before committed time, customer get delighted and he expresses his satisfaction. This satisfaction provides good recognition within network of other customers and hence new enquiries keep pouring!

When the business is new and just launched, you possess only a bare minimum capital if you are a sole owner of the business! If a new business is started by a seasoned entrepreneur, a certain sum of business capital is made available from money received from investors!

When business keep growing because of sales of product, capital starts building! Organization converts itself into proprietorship to private firm! Once the status of private limited firm is also going to change, organization look after becoming a public firm!

A public firm is an organization which has good market share and it can be in the business for several years! Organization offers its part of share capital for investment to institutional as well as retail investors! Institutional investors are basically large financial firms who are willing to fund the organization to carry out business operations. As a part of return on their investment, they get agreed sum after accounting of particular financial year! Institutional investors forms major part of the share capital after stakes of promoters!

21.3 Stock Exchange Listing Criteria

Any company, when decide to become a public organization so that they can raise the capital through investment from public domain, they have to fulfill some requirements of entry. India has two stock market exchanges which are known as National Stock Exchange – NSE and Bombay Stock Exchange – BSE! Following excerpts are referred from National Stock Exchange literature for sake of presentation of requirements. Since these are requirements, these are written as they are mentioned on NSE website for reference! These requirements are as follows:

A) Listing for SME on NSE, India.

Conditions precedent to listing

The issuers on SME platform shall have adhered to conditions precedent to listing as emerging, inter alia from

1. Securities Contracts (Regulations) Act 1956
2. Companies Act ,1956

3. Securities and Exchange Board of India Act, 1992
4. Any rules and/or regulations framed under foregoing statutes , as also any circular , clarifications, guidelines issued by the appropriate authority under foregoing statutes

Now let us see, eligibility criteria for listing on NSE emerge platform.

Incorporation:

The Issuer should be a company incorporated under the Companies Act 1956 / 2013 in India.

Post Issue Paid Up Capital:

The post issue paid up capital of the company (face value) shall not be more than Rs. 25 crore.

Track Record:

Track record of at least three years of either

i. the applicant seeking listing; or

ii. the promoters /promoting company, incorporated in or outside India or

iii.Proprietary / Partnership firm and subsequently converted into a Company (not in existence as a Company for three years) and approaches the Exchange for listing.

(Promoters mean one or more persons with minimum 3 years of experience in the same line of business and shall be holding at least 20% of the post issue equity share capital individually or severally.)

The company/entity should have operating profit (earnings before interest, depreciation and tax) from operations for at least any 2 out of 3 financial years preceding the application and its net-worth should be positive.

Other Listing Conditions:

i) The applicant company has not been referred to erstwhile Board for Industrial

ii) and Financial Reconstruction (BIFR) or No proceedings have been admitted under Insolvency and Bankruptcy Code against the issuer and Promoting companies

iii) The company has not received any winding up petition admitted by a NCLT / Court.

iv) No material regulatory or disciplinary action by a stock exchange or regulatory authority in the past three years against the applicant company.

Disclosures:

The following matters should be disclosed in the offer document:

1. Any material regulatory or disciplinary action by a stock exchange or regulatory authority in the past one year in respect of promoters/promoting company(ies), group companies, companies promoted by the promoters/promoting company(ies) of the applicant company.

2. Defaults in respect of payment of interest and/or principal to the debenture/bond/fixed deposit holders, banks, FIs by the applicant, promoters/promoting company(ies), group companies, companies promoted by the promoters/promoting company(ies) during the past three years.

3. The applicant, promoters/promoting company(ies), group companies, companies promoted by the promoters/promoting company(ies) litigation record, the nature of litigation, and status of litigation.

4. In respect of the track record of the directors, the status of criminal cases filed or nature of the investigation being undertaken with regard to alleged commission of any offence by any of its directors and its effect on the business of the company, where all or any of the directors of issuer have or has been charge-sheeted

with serious crimes like murder, rape, forgery, economic offences.

Reference: nseindia.com

B) Listing for Technology Start-Ups on NSE, India.

Conditions Precedent to Listing

The Issuers on SME platform shall have adhered to conditions precedent to listing as emerging, inter-alia, from

1. Securities Contracts (Regulations) Act 1956,
2. Companies Act 1956,
3. Securities and Exchange Board of India Act 1992,
4. Any rules and/or regulations framed under foregoing statutes, as also any circular, clarifications, guidelines issued by the appropriate authority under foregoing statutes.

Eligibility criteria for listing on NSE SME Platform for Technology start-ups

The following criteria should be complied with technology start-ups with as on the date of filing the Public Offer Document with NSE as well as when the same is filed with RoC and SEBI.

Incorporation:

The Issuer should be a company incorporated under the Companies Act 1956 / 2013 in India.

Post Issue Paid Up Capital:

The post issue paid up capital of the company (face value) shall not be more than Rs. 25 crore.

Track Record:

Track record of at least three years of either

i. the applicant seeking listing; or

ii. the promoters /promoting company, incorporated in or outside India or

iii. Proprietary / Partnership firm and subsequently converted into a Company (not in existence as a Company for three years) and approaches the Exchange for listing.

(Promoters mean one or more persons with minimum 3 years of experience in the same line of business and shall be holding at least 20% of the post issue equity share capital individually or severally.)

The company should have annual revenue of not less than Rs. 10 crores and should have shown an annual growth of at least 20% in the past one year. (Annual growth may in the form of number of users/revenue growth/customer base). The net-worth should be positive.

Optional Shareholding Conditions equivalent to track record:

i) At least 10% of its pre-issue capital to be held by qualified institutional buyer(s) (QIB) as on the date of filing of draft offer document.

ii) At least 10% of its pre-issue capital should be held by a member of the angel investor network or Private Equity Firms and Such angel investor network or Private Equity should have had an Investment in the start-up ecosystem in 25 or more start-ups their aggregate investment is more than 50 crores as on the date of filing of draft offer document.

Other Listing Conditions:

i) The applicant Company has not been referred to erstwhile Board for Industrial and Financial Reconstruction (BIFR).

ii) No petition for winding up is admitted by a Court of competent jurisdiction against the applicant Company.

iii) No material regulatory or disciplinary action by a stock exchange or regulatory authority in the past three years against the applicant company.

Disclosures:

The following matters should be disclosed in the offer document:

1. Any material regulatory or disciplinary action by a stock exchange or regulatory authority in the past one year in respect of promoters/promoting company(ies), group companies, companies promoted by the promoters/promoting company(ies) of the applicant company.

2. Defaults in respect of payment of interest and/or principal to the debenture/bond/fixed deposit holders, banks, FIs by the applicant, promoters/promoting company(ies), group companies, companies promoted by the promoters/promoting company(ies) during the past three years. An auditor's certificate shall also be provided by the issuer to the exchange, in this regard.

3. The applicant, promoters/promoting company(ies), group companies, companies promoted by the promoters/promoting company(ies) litigation record, the nature of litigation, and status of litigation.

4. In respect of the track record of the directors, the status of criminal cases filed or nature of the investigation being undertaken with regard to alleged commission of any offence by any of its directors and its effect on the business of the company, where all or any of the directors of issuer have or has been charge-sheeted with serious crimes like murder, rape, forgery, economic offences etc.

Reference: nseindia.com

C) Listing for Emerge Institutional Trading Platform (ITP) on NSE, India.

Conditions Precedent to Listing

The Issuers on SME platform shall have adhered to conditions precedent to listing as emerging, inter-alia, from

1. Securities Contracts (Regulations) Act 1956,
2. Companies Act 2013,
3. Securities and Exchange Board of India Act 1992,
4. Any rules and/or regulations framed under foregoing statutes, as also any circular, clarifications, guidelines issued by the appropriate authority under foregoing statutes.

Eligibility criteria for listing on NSE Emerge ITP Platform

The following criteria should be complied with as on the date of filing the Offer Document with NSE.

Eligibility Criteria

The following entities shall be eligible for listing on the institutional trading platform,-

1. an entity which is intensive in the use of technology, information technology,

intellectual property, data analytics, bio-technology or Nano-technology to provide products, services or business platforms with substantial value addition and at least twenty five per cent of its pre-issue capital is held by qualified institutional buyer(s) as on the date of filing of draft information document or draft offer document with the Board, as the case may be; or

2. any other entity in which at least fifty per cent of the pre-issue capital is held by qualified institutional buyers as on the date of filing of draft information document or draft offer document with the Board, as the case may be.

Other Listing Conditions:

1. The company, its promoter, group company or director does not appear in the wilful defaulters list of Reserve Bank of India as maintained by Credit Information Bureau (India) Limited;

2. There is no winding up petition against the company that has been admitted by a competent court;

3. The company, group companies or subsidiaries have not been referred to the Board for Industrial and Financial Reconstruction within a period of five years prior to the date of application for listing;

4. No regulatory action has been taken against the company, its promoter or director by SEBI, Reserve Bank of India, Insurance Regulatory and Development Authority or Ministry of Corporate Affairs within a period of five years prior to the date of application for listing;

Disclosures:

The following matters should be disclosed in the offer document:

1. Defaults in respect of payment of interest and/or principal to the debenture/bond/fixed deposit holders, banks, FIs by the applicant, promoters/promoting company(ies), group companies, companies promoted by the promoters/promoting company(ies) during the past three years. An auditor's certificate shall also be provided by the issuer to the exchange, in this regard.

2. The applicant, promoters/promoting company(ies), group companies, companies promoted by the promoters/promoting company(ies) litigation record, the nature of litigation, and status of litigation.

3. In respect of the track record of the directors, the status of criminal cases filed or nature of the investigation being undertaken with regard to alleged commission of any offence by any of its directors and its effect on the business of the company, where all or any of

the directors of issuer have or has been charge-sheeted with serious crimes like murder, rape, forgery, economic offences etc.

Reference: nseindia.com

D) Qualification for Listing IPO (Initial Public Offering)

Qualifications for listing Initial Public Offerings (IPO) are as below:

1. Paid up Capital

The paid-up equity capital of the applicant shall not be less than 10 crores and the capitalization of the applicant's equity shall not be less than 25 crores

Explanation 1

For this purpose, the post issue paid up equity capital for which listing is sought shall be taken

into account.

Explanation 2

For this purpose, capitalisation will be the product of the issue price and the post issue number of equity shares. In respect of the requirement of paid-up capital and market capitalisation, the issuers shall be required to include, in the disclaimer clause of the Exchange required to put in the offer document, that in the event of the market capitalisation (Product of issue price and the post issue number of shares) requirement of the Exchange not being met, the securities would not be listed on the Exchange.

2. Conditions Precedent to Listing:

The Issuer shall have adhered to conditions precedent to listing as emerging from inter-alia from Securities Contracts (Regulations) Act 1956, Companies Act 1956/2013, Securities and Exchange Board of India Act 1992, any rules and/or regulations framed under foregoing statutes, as also any circular, clarifications, guidelines issued by the appropriate authority under foregoing statutes.

At least three years track record of either:

i) The applicant seeking listing; or

ii) The promoters/promoting company, incorporated in or outside India or

iii) Partnership firm and subsequently converted into a Company (not in existence as a Company for three years) and approaches the Exchange for listing. The Company subsequently formed would be considered for listing only on fulfilment of conditions stipulated by SEBI in this regard.

For this purpose, the applicant or the promoting company shall submit annual reports of three preceding financial years to NSE and also provide a certificate to the Exchange in respect of the following:

iv) That the company has not referred to the Board of Industrial & Financial Reconstruction (BIFR) &/OR No proceedings have been admitted under Insolvency and Bankruptcy Code against the issuer and Promoting companies.

v) The company has not received any winding up petition admitted by a NCLT

vi) The net worth of the company should be positive. (Provided this criteria shall not be applicable to companies whose proposed issue size is more than Rs.500 crores)

[Net Worth – as defined under SEBI (Issue of Capital and Disclosure Requirements) Regulations, 2018.

Promoters mean one or more persons with minimum 3 years of experience of each of them in the same line of business and shall be holding at least 20% of the post issue equity share capital individually or severally.

The applicant desirous of listing its securities should satisfy the exchange on the following:

Redressal Mechanism of Investor grievance

The points of consideration are:

1. Details of pending investor grievances against Issuer, listed subsidiaries and top 5 listed group companies by Market Cap.
2. Arrangements or mechanism evolved for redressal of investor grievances including through SEBI Complaints Redressal System.

Defaults in payment

Defaults in respect of payment of interest and/or principal to the debenture/bond/fixed deposit holders by the applicant, promoters/promoting company (ies), group companies, Subsidiary Companies shall also be considered while evaluating a company's application for listing. The securities of the applicant company may not be listed till such time it has cleared all pending obligations relating to the payment of interest and/or principal.

Note: a)
In case a company approaches the Exchange for listing within six months of an IPO, the securities may be considered as eligible for listing if they were otherwise eligible for listing at the time of the IPO. If the company approaches the Exchange for listing after six months of an IPO, the norms for existing listed companies may be applied and market capitalisation be computed based on the period from the IPO to the time of listing.

Reference: nseindia.com

21.4 Listing Fees: (Applicable From April 2012)

There are various fees applicable for listing a company on NSE. The fee structure is as follow:

1) Processing Fees – 25,000
2) Initial Listing Fees – 25,000

Annual Listing Fees (Based on Paid Up capital)

1) Upto 5 Cr – 10,000
2) Between 5 Cr- 10 Cr – 15,000
3) Between 10 Cr – 20 Cr – 25,000
4) Between 20 Cr – 25 Cr – 45,000

Reference: nseindia.com

21.5 Listing Procedure on Bombay Stock Exchange- BSE for SME

Planning:

The Issuer Company consults and appoints the Merchant Banker/s in an advisory capacity.

Preparation:

The Merchant Banker prepares the documentation for filing after:

i) conducting due diligence regarding the Company i.e. checking the documentation including all the financial documents, material contracts, Government Approvals, Promoter details etc.

ii) and planning the IPO structure, share issuances, and financial requirements

Process:

Application procedure:

i) Submission of DRHP/Draft Prospectus - These documents are prepared by the Merchant Banker and filed with the Exchange as well as with SEBI as per requirements.
ii) Verification & Site Visit - BSE verifies the documents and processes the same. A visit to

the company's site shall be undertaken by the Exchange official .The Promoters are called for an interview with the Listing Advisory Committee.

iii) Approval - BSE issues an In Principle approval on the recommendation of the Committee, provided all the requirements are compiled by the Issuer Company. Filing of RHP/Prospectus - Merchant Banker files these documents with the ROC indicating the opening and closing date of the issue .Once approval is received from the ROC, they intimate the Exchange regarding the opening dates of the issue along with the required documents.

Public Offering:

The Initial Public Offer opens and closes as per schedule. After the closure of IPO, the Company submits the documents as per the checklist to the Exchange for finalization of the basis of allotment.

Post Listing:

BSE finalizes the basis of allotment and issues the Notice regarding Listing and Trading.

Reference: bsesme.com

21.6 Listing Fees on BSE (For FY 2023-24)

Following fee structure is followed before listing a company on BSE based on value of paid up capital.

Paid up capital is the amount of money company has received from shareholders in exchange for shares of stock.

1) Initial Listing Fees – 20,000

   Upto 100 Cr, For Exclusively Listed Companies – 3, 25,000

2) Upto 100 Cr – For Commonly listed companies – 2,85,000

3) Above 100 Cr and Upto 200 Cr – 3,60,000 Rs

4) Above 200 Cr and Upto 300 Cr – 4,65,000 Rs

5) Above 300 Cr and Upto 400 Cr – 5,65,000 Rs

6) Above 400 Cr and Upto 500 Cr – 6,95,000 Rs

7) Above 500 Cr and Upto 1000 Cr-

   Rs.7, 00,000/- and an additional listing fee of Rs. 4,560/- for every increase of Rs. 5 crores or part thereof above 500 crores in the paid up share capital

8) Above 1000 Cr - Rs.11, 60,000/- and an additional listing fee of Rs.4, 870/- for every increase of Rs. 5 crores or part thereof above 1,000 crores in the paid up share capital.

Reference: bseindia.com

21.7 How a person can buy a share:

Requirements for entering into capital market for selling and buying of stocks are:

1) The investors must have a valid PAN card.

2) The investor must have a bank account in which a demat account is linked to it. Demat account is special account which is used for capital market related transactions.

3) The next step is look for SEBI registered broker, fill up KYC form and enters into broker –client agreement.

4) The broker will allocate unique client ID which will be used for authentication.

5) Now securities can by bought or sold!

Reference: nseindia.com

Often buying and selling share has a certain brokerage amount as service charge give to brokers. Every investor has to study an investment friendly company before investing their hardly earned money.

21.8 How one can purchase Investment Products?

If you are competent enough to trade in securities market with the help of broker, it's good. If you don't have sufficient knowledge, time and experience, you can always reach out to professional and buy their investment product and focus on your normal work till the completion of maturity period of that investment product.

Some of the investment products and their sellers:

1) **Broker:** Brokers offer several services like purchase /sale of equity, debt and derivative products, mutual fund units, IPO's etc. .

2) Banks : Bank also offer above mentioned investment products both physically and on their respective websites.

3) Mutual Funds : There are several mutual fund selling organizations . One can avail their services by reaching them physically as well as on their dedicated websites.

4) Stock Exchanges : Closed end and open ended mutual funds are traded on stock exchanges . One can buy these products from these stock exchanges .

Reference : nseindia.com

21.9 What are Mutual Funds ?

A mutual fund is a company that pools money from many investors and invest into other investment products which gives good to fair amount of returns on the basis of short term , medium term and long term market performance and relevant investments .

Mutual fund invests the money into purchase of stocks , purchase of bonds and financing short term debt . The combined holding in a mutual fund is known as its portfolio . Every investor purchase shares from mutual fund . The price of share indicates the income generated . This price keep changing based on market performance. Hence if you are buying a mutual fund by investing some X amount , on that day whatever is the value of share , you will get relevant units . If after two three years , the share prices go up and you decide to sell the units , you will get relevant return according to value of the shares . If after two three year , the share value decreases, the loss will be created. Hence mutual funds are subject to market risk . One should invest in mutual funds based on their study , diversification strategies, sector performance , fund managers professional expertise , market fluctuations. Buying and selling decisions of mutual funds are market driven , so one has to stay updated to know about the market trends.

The Net Asset Value is the value of your investment and it keeps changing based on market performance . Buying mutual funds when NAV is less , will give you more units . Buying mutual funds when NAV is more ,will give you less units .

Mutual funds are professionally managed funds . Many fund managers has diverse experience of investment market , financial decision making and trends in capital market . Accordingly they devise investment strategies and search to give considerable returns on investor's investment . The job of fund managers is also to assess and analyse the risk in investment market and refrain investors from investing in risky funds . Diversification is carried out to reduce the effect of market up and downs . Mutual funds are highly affordable as well as they are highly liquid . One can sell or buy them by providing the processing fees.

Locking period is the time where you cannot withdraw your investments for pre decided time interval ! After completion of locking period, you can withdraw the money ! This is done to ensure money remain constantly available in financial market so that capital building decisions can be taken reliably !

There are high risk funds also where investments are done in riskier stocks . Riskier stocks have a benefit that if market is supportive , the returns are extremely higher . So , if someone is ready to take the risk of investment to a calculated amount , they can buy short term high risk mutual funds which give huge returns in short time if market performance is good to great !

Mutual fund invests their money in different sectors , so that they can get its benefit . Different investment sectors are money market funds , bond funds, and stock funds ! Stock funds are further divided into growth funds , income funds, index funds and sector funds !

When mutual fund gives return it gives in the form of major benefits. Benefits of mutual funds are received in the form of payment of dividend, distribution of capital gain , higher value of NAV !

The risk associated with mutual funds are change in value of funds , market volatility and investors risk averse nature . People sell shares if more volatility is seen ,which decreases value of the fund and NAV ! Because of major market up-down , dividend and interest payout is also become impossible . In such cases , investors face losses . So, it is always advisable to study the past performance of the fund to analyse the overall stability of the fund and number of regular investors .

For buying and selling mutual funds and looking for their management in investment market , fund managers work seamlessly . There are operating expenses of mutual funds and same are covered as fees of mutual funds . The fees are charged based on certain percentage to invested amount for respective tenure . E.g. Annual operating expenses of 1%, 0.5%, 1.5 % etc. . Higher the value of operating fee, less is the value of mutual fund in future . So, one has to take care of noting the expenses fees before investing into mutual funds .

Mutual fund prospectus and shareholders report need to share with statutory authorities . Additionally , investment advisers who are registers with statutory authorities manages portfolio of mutual fund ! One has to check these essential things before investment !

Mutual Fund Examples with annualized three year returns :

1) Axis Blue-chip Fund - 18.88 %

2) Mirae Asset Large Cap Fund – 25.61 %

3) Parag Parikh Long Term Equity Fund – 32.38 %

4) UTI Flexi Cap Fund – 24.07 %

5) Axis Midcap Fund – 25.19 %

6) Kotak Emerging Equity Fund – 36.06%

7) Axis Small Cap Fund – 38.17 %

8) SBI Small Cap Fund – 39.05 %

9) SBI Equity Hybrid Fund – 19.96 %

10) Mirae Asset Hybrid Equity Fund – 21.86 %

So , rupees 1 Lakh invested in Axis Blue-chip Fund three years ago will yield 1.68 Lakh today ! Giving almost 68 % returns on one time pay !

Mutual fund investments can be done per month also starting from small amount as 10 Rs ! The logic is , more the number of investors , more will be the fund value and more money will be available as capital !

References : groww.in , investor.gov

21.10 Terms related to Shares :

1) Share - A share is the interest of a member in a company as per company law . The interest is indicated in the form of number of shares a particular shareholder owns .

2) Book Value of Share – It is the value of share shareholder will theoretically get if the company is liquidated . Market value of the share can be higher or lower . Accordingly an interested buyer will buy or sell the shares .

3) Face Value of the Share – It is the price at which one can purchase the shares. It's the value mentioned in share certificates .

4) Ordinary Shares or Equity Shares – These are common type of shares with voting rights to shareholder . However shareholders cannot receive nor demand dividends on shares.

5) Preference Shares – Preference shares gives preferential rights to shareholders. Shareholders can receive dividends and they also can get their invested capital back when company is liquidated.

6) Redeemable Preference Shares – These shares can be exchanged in return of cash .

7) Non-Redeemable Preference Shares – These shares cannot be exchanged . They can be obtained only during liquidation of company assets .

8) Convertible Preference Shares – These shares gives fixed amount of dividend for a particular time period. Once this period is over , they can be converted into ordinary shares or can be kept as it is !

9) Treasury Shares : These are shares acquired by the company from shareholders. The proportion of treasury shares should not be more than 10 % to ordinary shares !

10) Indian Depository Receipts : This is a financial instrument denominated in Indian Rupees in the form of depository receipts created by a domestic depository (custodian of securities registered with the securities and exchange board of India !) against the underlying equity of issuing company to enable foreign companies to raise funds from the Indian securities market .

11) Debentures : It's the long term business debt not secured by any collateral . Its funding option for companies with solid finances that want to avoid issuing shares and diluting their equity .

12) Fully Convertible Debentures : It's a type of debt security in which the entire value is convertible into equity shares at the issuer's notice .

13) Partially Convertible Debentures: It's the debt instrument where after completion of specific period investor can convert some portion into equity shares of the company .

14) Amortization : Amortization is an accounting technique used to periodically lower the book value of loan or an intangible asset over a set period of time .

15) Depreciation : Depreciation is an accounting technique in which cost of tangible or physical assets over its useful life is calculated.

Reference : Wikipedia

21.11 Share Trading Examples:

Many share broker and investment professionals guide investors from time to time about investment decisions in particular shares . The selling or buying decision is communicated based on share trends observed in market . Before giving suggestion of selling and buying shares , target value is indicated . The minimum time in which share achieves that price is the moment of transaction . If delayed , share price may change subsequently . Because it's a market judgment ! So best strategy to invest in shares is study these advises and apply your own judgment and funding amount ! When a required profit is booked , new shares can be purchased and same can be sold once target price is achieved .

Reference : iepf.gov.in , sebi.gov.in, 5paisa.com

21.12 Study of Balance sheet of company before investing in shares :

1) Read the balance sheet as it is presented in press note , its public sharing done on periodic basic . Usually , after every quarter end ,

company performance is presented with the help of balance sheet.

2) Balance sheet is combination of asset and liabilities of companies .

3) Balance sheet analyse expenses occurred on procurement of material , payment of salaries, procurement of machines .

4) Balance sheet note sales done in certain time period , it calculates near business earnings by subtracting expenses from incomes .

5) Net positive value of Income minus expense indicates profit while net negative value indicates loss of the business.

6) Loss making company cannot survive in market because of financial constraints and increase in liabilities .

7) Asset building company is growth oriented company as assets are created by investing money from business profit .

8) Loan or debt component of business is specifically indicated in balance sheet and a no

loan company raises capital on their own or through equity shares .

9) Profit to earnings ratio is crucial and a higher P/E ratio indicates higher growth . Investing in growth oriented organization indicates better chances to get higher returns .

10) Company balance sheet can be refereed to quarter to quarter or this year's quarter to last year's quarter to understand the business dynamics and investment growth .

11) A steady rise in business profit is good indicator and hence investor can safely invest in such organization .

12) The percentage of equity shares, preferential shares , debentures , amortization , depreciation values are important . It helps to relate how financial health of the company is maintained .

13) Shareholders complaint's and their resolution is indicated in annual general meeting report . This also needs to review before investing . Buying and selling shares is done after

study of declaration of earnings, dividends ! This gives clear idea for decision making .

21.13 Company Liquidation Process :

Its tough call for any organization but sometimes prevailing scenarios indicates a possibility of suitable decisions to pay the liabilities.

Insolvency is a business term in which company fails to attain required level of profit . Because of no profit , business operations and creditors payment become a challenge to owners and there are chances of default of payment . In such cases , when creditors payment default to such an extent that the recovery is possible only after selling of assets of the company , at that moment , process of liquidation starts.

Liquidation happens in three ways :

1) **Voluntary liquidation** – It's not a forcible decision , its decision of owner and company is in a position to pay for creditors.

2)   Creditors Voluntary liquidation – It's the type of liquidation when owner realizes it's going to have default in creditors payment and hence the liquidate the assets of the company to pay for creditors .

3) Compulsory liquidation   : This type of liquidation happens because of order from court of law or order issuing authority . Business is not able to pay for liabilities and hence it is to be terminated .

Sequence of Liquidation :

1)   The main cause of liquidation is financial liability which is referred as insolvency and bankruptcy . The financial condition is assessed by adjudicating authority and resolution plan is provided by company . The plan is approved by adjudicating authority and liquidation order is given as per prescribed time limit .

2) The adjudicating authority can reject resolution plan and give liquidation order because of multiple reasons.

3) If the committee of creditors approves the corporate debtors to liquidate , the liquidation order is given .

4) If the approved resolution plan is contradicted by corporate debtor , liquidation order is given .

5) With the help of liquidation order and appointment of registered liquidator with adjudicating authority , the process of liquidation starts . The liquidator is supposed to fill the position till complete process of liquidation . He or she can be replaced any time by adjudicating authority . He or she need to qualify the requirement of Insolvency and Bankruptcy code !

6) Excluding cash and bank balances, company assets are sold as per necessity and priority , one by one and financial liabilities are paid off .

7)   The debt liabilities are first paid off . Remaining amount is paid to different creditors as per set pre –established orders . Companies Secure creditors are paid first followed by preferential creditors like payment of government taxes, employee salaries .

8)   The next payment is done for debenture holders and for other miscellaneous liabilities by floating charge on all assets . After that unsecured creditors and preference shareholders are paid off.

9)   Finally , if remaining sum is surplus , it is equally distributed with shareholders as per pre-established order . If its deficit , shareholders is asked to pay the unpaid share capital .

10)   This is how winding up of company takes place depending on nature of complexity , business scenario and insolvency causes. Once liquidation process is completed , the company is cease to exist as per law !

11) Companies can be liquidated or they can be converted to limited liability Company as LLP ! Business liability is nothing but financial trust of investors before funding in the company in the form of several financial instruments.

Reference : mca.gov.in , resurgentindia.com

21.14 Leading Share markets across the globe :

A) Trillion USD club

- BSE India Limited
- National Stock Exchange Of India
- NASDAQ –US
- NYSE
- TMX Group
- London Stock Exchange
- Euronext
- NASDAQ OMX Nordic Exchange
- Deutsche Boerse
- Six Swiss Exchange
- Shanghai Stock Exchange

- Korea Exchange
- Japan Exchange Group
- Hong Kong Exchanges and Clearing
- SHENZHEN Stock Exchange
- Australian Securities Exchange

B) Region wise 60 Stock Markets with their market capital :

Asian Stock Markets :

Total Numbers : 17

Total Values : 23,048 Billion USD

Percentage of Worlds total : 33.3 %

1. BSE India Limited – 1482 Bn $
2. National Stock Exchange of India – 1450 Bn $
3. Colombo Stock Exchange – 21 Bn $
4. Shanghai Stock Exchange – 4460 Bn $
5. Shenzhen Stock Exchange – 3424 Bn $

6. Hong Kong Exchanges and Clearing – 3165 Bn $

7. Taipei Exchange – 82 Bn $

8. Taiwan Stock Exchange Corp – 750 Bn $

9. Korea Exchange – 1265 Bn $

10. Japan Exchange Group – 4910 Bn $

11. Stock Exchange of Thailand – 368 Bn $

12. Philippine Stock Exchange – 238 Bn $

13. Ho Chi Minh Stock Exchange – 50 Bn $

14. Singapore Exchange – 639 Bn $

15. Bursa Malaysia – 380 Bn $

16. Indonesia Stock Market – 347 Bn $

17. Kazakhstan Stock Market – 39 Bn $

Australia- New Zealand Stock Markets:

Total Numbers : 2

Total Values : 1207 Billion USD

Percentage of Worlds total : 1.75 %

1. Australian Securities Exchange – 1139 Bn $
2. NZX Limited – 68 Bn $

Europe's Stock Markets :

Total Numbers : 17

Total Values : 13589 Billion USD

Percentage of Worlds total : 19.5 %

1. Euronext – 3379 Bn $
2. London Stock Exchange – 3272 Bn $
3. Irish Stock Exchange – 134 Bn $
4. Deutsche Boerse – 1738 Bn $
5. Six Swiss Exchange – 1479 Bn $
6. Luxembourg Stock Exchange – 49 Bn $
7. Oslo Bors – 201 Bn $
8. Moscow Exchange – 447 Bn $
9. NASDAQ OMX Nordic Exchange – 1253 Bn $
10. Wiener Borse – 96 Bn $
11. Budapest Stock Exchange – 17 Bn $

12. Ljubljana Stock Exchange – 6 Bn $

13. Borsa Italia – 653 Bn $

14. Malta Stock Exchange – 4 Bn $

15. BME Spanish Exchanges – 833 Bn $

16. Athens Stock Exchange – 27 Bn $

17. Cyprus Stock Exchange – 3 Bn $

African Stock Market :

Total Numbers : 5

Total Values : 1122 Billion USD

Percentage of Worlds total : 1.5 %

1. Johannesburg Stock Exchange - 790 Bn $

2. Nigerian Stock Exchange – 47 Bn $

3. Egyptian Exchange – 53 Bn $

4. Bourse de Casablanca – 46 Bn $

5. Stock Exchange of Mauritius – 7 Bn $

Middle East Stock Markets :

Total Numbers : 9

Total Values : 1410 Billion USD

Percentage of Worlds total : 2 %

1. Saudi Stock Exchange (Tadawul) -442 Bn $
2. Qatar Stock Exchange – 146 Bn $
3. Abu Dhabi Securities Exchange – 110 Bn $
4. Muscat Securities Market – 38 Bn $
5. Dubai Financial Market – 87 Bn $
6. Qatar Stock Exchange – 146 Bn $
7. Bahrain Bourse – 20 Bn $
8. Borsa Istanbul – 197 Bn $
9. Tel-Aviv Stock Exchange – 237 Bn $

North American Stock Market :

Total Numbers : 5

Total Values : 28059 Billion USD

Percentage of Worlds total : 40.6 %

1. NYSE – New York Stock Exchange – 18486 Bn $

2. NASDAQ US – 7449 Bn $

3. TMX Group – 1697 Bn $

4. Bolsa Mexicana de Valores – 426 Bn $

5. Bermuda Stock Exchange – 1 Bn $

South American Stock Market :

Total Numbers : 5

Total Values : 933 Billion USD

Percentage of Worlds total : 1.35 %

1. BM & F BOVESPA – 519 Bn $

2. Bolsa de Comercio de Santiago – 187 Bn $

3. Bolsa de Comercio de Buenos Aires – 81 Bn $

4. Bolsa de Valores de Lima – 58 Bn $

5. Bolsa de Valores de Colombia – 88 Bn $

(*Reference* : Visualcapitalist.com)

21.15 Conflict Of Interest

In stock market , the stocks get sold through brokers . Brokers have good amount of knowledge about whatever movement happening in share market . This information has to be passed correctly and brokers are supposed to indicate actual sale and buy price for investors.

In achieving short position , sometime a hype is created in market about a particular share and it is rumored that the respective shares are going to rise in quick time so that investors can book good profit . With this new , people buy such stocks and it create high demand for those stocks because of which price go up and up . In this way brokers attain high level of share price and good brokerage . In other rumor , the prices of stock are suggested to be reduced because of low performance of the firm

. People start to sell those stocks and again a demand for selling increases . When people sell , they don't go for more negotiation , they just want to get their money back quickly . This selling make bunch of stock available with stock market and which are again traded by creating hype in the market ! Compromise with primary interest of providing correct stock knowledge to investors at an agreed brokerage against the secondary interest of earning profit and brokerage from transaction is known as conflict of interest .

The transparency in the system gets affected because of conflict of interest . There are many organizations who don't allow certain people to participate in financial decision making because of conflict of interest . When you have to take impartial decision for the benefit of organization , you have to take some harsh calls. Hence organizations are professionally managed . Other kind of moral or external pressure in not considered . Decisions of financial acumen are taken with the help of suggested process guidelines !

So , every investor should study the company they are investing before making any buy or sell decision ! Conflict of Interest of brokers, organization and self-need to be noted.

21.16 Annual General Meeting :

Annual General Meeting is the annual meeting held by an organization for its interested shareholders. Time , Date and venue of the meeting are communicated in advance to respective shareholders through press note ! The purpose of Annual general meeting is to present the financial statements of the company in front of the shareholders and to present the vision of the company about future plans .

In AGM following activities are carried out with the presence of shareholders having voting rights . Votes can be casted by proxy voting through e-mail or by post !

1)   Company appoints board of directors and gets their appointment approved from its shareholders.

2)   Shareholders votes in favor or in oppose in this meeting !

3)   Company presents financial performance of the year and gets approved from shareholders . Minutes of last year's annual general meeting are also approved .

4)   The compensation of the executives is declared and approved by the shareholders.

5)   Appointment of Auditors is announced and approved with shareholders votes .

6)   Company directors express their vision about future development in the organization . In AGM , directors give time for answering questions asked by shareholders on any present issue . They provide satisfactory explanation about the status of the issues.

7)   Announcement of dividend is also approved in the AGM by shareholders .

8)   Minutes of AGM are communicated via press note as a general information . Same is also provided to regulatory authorities for their information .

9)   Shareholders may ask to company directors about the low performance of the

company in case company experiencing some challenges . If company is taking some business decisions such as acquisition , mergers , shareholders have a right to express their concerns over such developments .

10) Annual General Meeting is symbol of yearlong performance of the company in front of its lakhs of shareholders . Financial results

express the effect of professional management of business operations that meet customer need and produce profit for the company which is important for long term running of business activities !

21.17 Business Strategies :

The stock market responds differently to different business strategies implemented by directors in order to either keep business in tact or make business more profitable . The basic aim of implementing business strategies is to take care of the company to avoid liquidation or bankruptcy and to ensure people maintain their jobs . Even after implementing such strategies , if business fails to recover , then such company marches towards liquidation process.

a) **Acquisition** : Company acquires other company at a purchase price . In this acquisition Seller Company hand over all its share to new company . The staff working for the seller company may remain same or new candidates can be added . The operations of the company are directed by new purchaser and profit earned is booked under new acquisition name of the company transferring complete ownership from previous owner to new owner .

b) Merger : Merger is also a business strategy in which ailing business is owned by other owner and companies rights , shares , resources are hand over to new owner at a sales price . The new owner adds his or her investment fund and develops company to new level of performance by adding staff, introducing new products and changing ways of working !

c) Tie Up or Collaboration : Organizations tie up with each other by distributing number of

shares proportionately . The main aim of tie up is to use each other resources for everyone's benefit . In tie up and collaboration , technology may be handed over , new machines can be supplied, new software's can be provided . After successful business performance , profit is shared as per agreed proportion .

An international company if wanted to spread in certain territory without investing in own resources , mainly technology tie ups are collaborated with domestic company by approaching each other . Domestic company uses that technical knowledge to improve its product features and sell them at higher price and to larger customers!

d) **Separation :** The way companies come together , in same fashion they separate from each other by distributing respective shares . In some cases , the separation also follows closure of business ! In some cases , one business get close while other partner run the business at their end . Leadership of business is very much important which decide how a typical company will perform in coming days ! Clear technical knowledge , ability to understand customer dire need and potential to sell it at lowest possible cost make a company profitable .

e) Diversification : The decision of diversification is nothing but creating different products in different customer segments . A company can produce oil , can produce vehicles , can produce software's and can produce beauty products under one group name ! This is known as diversification of the business. The main aim of the diversification is to remain relevant in market and serve larger customer to ensure business remain profitable . When companies carry out different diversification , the board of directors recruits specific executives having required expertise and they offer rights of selection of operational team to make that business perform well .

The other advantage of diversification is when one business sector is not performing well , the other business house perform well and maintain the business profit to required level ensuring seamless operations .

f) **Expansion :** Business expansion includes transforming business to a huge scale . A typical 100 Cr turnover company plans to expand itself to 10,000 Cr company in coming ten years systematically by opening 10 manufacturing facilities, 50 marketing offices , 4 training and development centers and 2 research and development centers ! With such a time bound plan every year the respective phase of expansion is carried out to meet the end goal of transformation .

Whenever companies are expanding , they invest heavily in business . The main aim of expansion is to leverage the in demand technology for making more profit . Suppose a businessman get a hint that in coming ten years there is requirement of minimum 5 lakhs electric car per years , will you expand ? He suddenly starts their calculations , contact interested investors , check the current shareholding status and take a well informed decision of expansion . Business expansion is not an easy process. You have to depute your key person to ensure transformation happens as per the practice and values cherished in the organization over the years . It takes some time for establishment of new business houses , but after passing period of two to three year , business get set properly !

With rise in financial capital , more shares can be made available for trading . With more transaction ,more capital chip in and in this way expansion process become fast pace and required results are achieved in ten years planned phase . Till the response from market is awaited , directors have to arrange communication drive for in future business expansions and they need to express their readiness for new investments from shareholders !

Shares and equity market has all these things which keep happening . Depending upon business performance , quarterly results changes . Economy of the nation is either booming or facing recession . In a booming economy , there is always a high demand for products and hence companies keep working relentlessly to meet those demands and earn profit . In recession , the demand is low and business houses struggle to get required business. In booming economy , share prices are higher . People don't sale the shares which are purchased . Share price keep rising and because of which shareholders get good return on their investment if they sell shares. In recession , share prices are falling , this is the best time to buy these shares for new investor having investment potential . When market recovers from recession , they get good returns ! Shareholders always need to be informed ! ⊛⊛

CHAPTER 22 : SOCIAL CORPORATE RESPONSE

" As far as society service is concerned , there is no upper limit. "

Image Courtesy: Trees on the beach , pixabay.com

22.1 Introduction :

Business is one of the way of earning ones livelihood . Natural resources when converted to useful form by applying technology of necessary conversion give rise to useful products which are sold in the market . The sold products generate revenues and make company profitable . Over the years , company goes on doing same task and keeps improving itself by developing new products for customers . Customer needs keep changing so as company invents new products that fulfill that need . How much money should be earned by a company has no limit in reality . As far as your products are getting sold and your competitors are also not influencing your operations and market share to larger degree , your business goes on . You make huge profit and thus grow your organization !

The growing success of your firm set yourself apart from other players in the market and now society see at you as a more responsible entity . People expect more contribution from your side for society upliftment . Even government has specified certain amount of profit sharing in corporate social responsibility activities . As per sec 135 of the companies act 2013 , 2% profit of last three preceding year has to invested in corporate social responsibility activities.

This gives scope for corporate social responsibility . Many companies who are large enough to contribute for society do their part and make surrounding   area more peaceful , vibrant and useful for society . In this chapter , efforts of CSR will be discussed along with its specific examples and its impact on nearby society !

22.2 Types of CSR :

There are predominantly four types of CSR activities which are carried out by corporates . These four types are :

A) Environmental Activities .

B) Ethical activities

C) Financial Activities .

D) Philanthropic Activities .

Let's discuss them one by one !

A) Environmental Activities :

Every company follows a quality assurance and control standards as well as safety standard to ensure the operations done in the premises are not harmful to each other and products also do not cause harm during their use ! Serving the environment in which we are working is prime duty and hence corporate social responsibility efforts get directed toward various environment protection drives such as –

i) Tree plantation in nearby area and its scheduled maintenance !

ii) Industrial farming and milk dairy support to local farmers . With this arrangement, company provides supporting hand to farmers for focusing on agro products and ensures they get sold to right market.

iii) Building solar power plant in nearby area for street lightening .

iv) Constructing roads in hilly terrain and ensure people use the facility of road for daily commute .

v) Avoiding pollution inside factory by implementing strict safety systems . Proper processing of waste material and keeping environment clean . Taking care of animal group by providing them their food .

B) Ethical Activities :

Business and ethics has close relation . How do you feel , when you get a product and receives its benefit for several years without any complaint ? You feel , whatever money you invested in purchasing the product is paid off ! This is the result of ethics of business !

Every business as starts growing , it takes more care about its brand image and its presence in society at large . With boost in sales of your product and because of their satisfactory performance at customer end , brand attains its recognition and become widely popular . Later on , products get sold just by referring to its brand name . This is the impact of ethics , your brand become identity of your success .

Companies ensure their interpersonal relation with every stakeholder is supportive and respectful . The staff , vendors and service providers feel inspired and happy while serving

. The decision taken in the organization is mutually beneficial and should follow proper justice to every stakeholders. If any business issue arises in front of people , company always take ethical stands and ensure the correct will be chosen. Good people deal with good people . In business also , ethical organization receives more business from reputed business , making business activities more simple to perform . Ethical CSR act as improvement measure in organizations environment .

C) Financial Activities :

As a part of financial CSR , company donates money in several social projects . Social projects are projects carried out by non-government organization to cater the need of deprived society . Running a school in underprivileged society is a dire need , but building a school , deputing necessary staff and making that school available to nearby student is big task which require financial support . Many companies support such schools and ensure people get quality education .

Company takes responsibilities of villages for its upliftment . They provide each and every facility either separately or along with local government to support the citizens .

Many companies provide medical support to deceased by donating ambulance service , building charity hospital and creating blood banks .

Providing grants and scholarships to successful student is also a good CSR . Company also sponsor sportsman for their contribution and for future journey .

Company create employment and most of the time , if talent is locally available , its recruited to uplift the locals !

D) Philanthropic Activities :

As far as society service is concerned , there is no upper limit. Our society needs good hearts that can feel the pain of others and provide a solution that relieves that pain .

Philanthropic activities include huge scale availability of social foundations that fulfill the need of poor's. There are lots of poor countries in the world and children's in such country don't get basic upbringing essentials . Through philanthropic actions , people reach there and provide these essentials in huge scale . When natural calamities occur , people provide support in the form of urgent aid and subsequent rehabilitation .

Philanthropy cannot be compared to government work but it is quite considerable ! Taking care of certain area for its medical need, education need, social security need all comes under umbrella of philanthropy .

22.3 How CSR set apart to a firm :

1) CSR builds brand image . When your brand is known for its contribution in society , people look at services offered differently . Every business needs several facets of its development . People side of business always encourages businesses to implement new initiatives in their society where they can participate and learn new things . CSR recognizes brand !

2) Benefits of CSR activities last long for local people . If some concrete work is done for the society , the generations over generation ripe those benefits and always provide a goodwill to organization because of which this become possible .

3) Financial aspects of business get improved . People believe in your commitment to provide a

quality atmosphere in nearby society . They notice , you are good at work and good at society also ! This keeps informal relation very very caring towards each other .

4) Among peers and competitors , effect of CSR multifolds . Other companies also take necessary steps and ensure they also contribute equally and to the best of their abilities . This creates a eco system of support where people coming from all walk of life support each other and takes care of each other !

5) 2% investment of profit is very very small expectation from businesses . If a business earns 100 Cr profit in preceding three years , it needs to spend just 2 Cr on CSR ! When a business is set , the profit from business is almost guaranteed . As far as people in the organization are humble and innovative , profit will keep pouring . With such small investment from large number of

corporates definitely improves society atmosphere !

22.4 ISO 26000 Standards for CSR initiatives

: ISO 26000 is defined as international standard developed to help organizations effectively assess and address social responsibilities that are relevant and significant to their mission and vision , operations and processes, customer , employees, communities and other stakeholders and environmental impact !

ISO 26000 focuses on 7 core subjects which are :

1) Issues concerned regarding to human rights are due diligence .
2) Human rights risk situations .
3) Avoidance of complicity .
4) Resolving grievances .
5) Discrimination and vulnerable groups .
6) Civil and political rights .

7) Fundamental principles and rights at work .

(*Reference* : iso.org)

22.5 Top 5 Companies in India with their CSR contribution in FY 2020-21 :

1) Godrej Consumer Product Limited : 34.08 Cr : Soonabai Pirojsha Godrej Foundation

CSR : Support to 9000 nano entrepreneurs, zero waste to landfill and water positivity , 100 % extended producers responsibility , A rating in climate disclosure project !

2) Infosys Limited : 325.32 Cr : Infosys Foundation

CSR : Infosys Head start initiative to provide digital and life skills to over 10 Million people by 2025 , believes in holistic community development , institution building and sustainability related initiatives .

3) Wipro Limited : 251 Cr : Wipro Foundation

CSR: Support to 1561 projects covering humanitarian aid, integrated healthcare support , livelihood regeneration , cumulatively reaching toward 10 million by COVID-19 response . Supported in providing food, dry ration , personal hygiene kits to over 10.2 million people , distributed 330 million meals , helped over 8.2 million people in livelihood generation and supported 500 non-profit organization in providing humanitarian and healthcare aids .

4) Tata Chemicals Limited : 21 Crorers

Aided 6878 farmers in capacity building, field demonstrations, livestock management, Connected 25190 artisians of okhai to customers , planted 1.15 lakhs mangroves in Mithapur .

5) ITC Limited : 353.46 Cr

Greened 30439 acres of land , supported 33000 children's in education , vocational training to 12470 students, supported in construction of 640 individual household toilets in 28 districts , through ' well-being out of waste –WOW' initiative collected 70900 MT dry waste from 1067 wards.

(*Ref :* thecsrjournal.in)

Note :

Additional Volumes :

Volume 2 : Chapters 23-30 , 1- 10 Quiz Sections

Volume 3 : 11-20 Quiz Sections

✳✳✳

VOLUME 1
COMPLETE

www.ingramcontent.com/pod-product-compliance
Lightning Source LLC
Chambersburg PA
CBHW071028290526
45795CB00004B/1147

* 9 7 9 8 8 8 0 1 2 4 9 6 1 *